Code this Game!

by **Meg Ray**

art by **Keith Zoo**

New York

To Silas—you were right, programming is fun.

Library of Congress Cataloging-in-Publication Data is available.

ISBN: 978-1-250-30669-2

WRITER Meg Ray   ILLUSTRATOR Keith Zoo
DESIGNER Timothy Hall   EDITOR Daniel Nayeri
FORMAT DESIGNER Phil Conigliaro   CODE VETTER Piper Thunstrom

Our books are available at special discounts when purchased in bulk for premiums and sales promotions as well as for fund-raising or educational use. Special editions or book excerpts also can be created to specification. For details, contact the Macmillan Corporate and Premium Sales Department at the address below, or send an email to MacmillanSpecialMarkets@macmillan.com.

DISCLAIMER
The publisher and authors disclaim responsibility for any loss, injury, or damages caused as a result of any of the instructions described in this book.

The code in this book was written by Meg Ray and is placed in the Mozilla Public License 2.0 (MPL-2.0) or the most recent version. So you may use, remix, and break it however you like.

An imprint of Macmillan Children's Publishing Group
120 Broadway, New York, NY 10271
OddDot.com

Printed in China by L. Rex Printing Company Limited,
Dongguan City, Guangdong Province

First edition, 2019

1 3 5 7 9 10 8 6 4 2

JOYFUL BOOKS
FOR **CURIOUS MINDS**

Contents

Part 1: Introduction

Part 2: Code This Game

Hello, world!

Part 3: Break This Game

How old are you?

I just turned 1001 in binary! *

* The binary number **1001** equals the decimal number **9**!

Part 1

Introduction

Meet Your Guide

Hi, I'm Meg. I'm here to help you develop your new coding skills. Look for me to cheer you on and give you the inside scoop on programming.

What to Do with This Book

Make Your Game!

Follow the tutorial to build a game called *Attack of the Vampire Pizzas!* This is a tower defense–style game. In tower defense games, you protect something from enemies by placing defenses. In *Attack of the Vampire Pizzas!*, you will use pizza toppings and tools to protect your delivery boxes from oncoming vampire pizzas.

You will learn the basics of programming (coding) in Python as you create the game.

Break Your Game!

Why would we want you to break the game that you just made? To make it your own!

You need to break this game to be able to play with it and make something new. But don't worry; you'll save a copy of the game before you break it.

Keep an Eye Out for These Sections

Power Up

Check out these quick tips to make things easier and get your code right.

New Words

These are your guide to the language of computer science. You'll be fluent in no time!

Level Up!
Keep track of your progress and successes as you master new coding skills.

Each chapter begins with the goals of the new feature you will be building.

Meg Hedgehog will guide you through building the new feature. Look out for these sections.

>>> Type This

Type This sections give you a snippet of new code to type into your program exactly as it is written. Look for code comments marked with a # in the code to tell you what each line of code does. You do not need to type the comments into your program.

Take a Closer Look

```
#Define the VampireSprite set-up method
    def __init__(self):
        super().__init__()
        self.speed = 2
        self.lane = randint (0, 4)
        all_vampires.add (self)
```

```
def __init__(self):
```

This section looks at **code** in detail to help you understand what it does.

▶ Your Turn

Your Turn sections ask you to figure things out on your own. Look for code comments marked **#To Do**. As you practice, the directions in this section will become less detailed.

Refactor

Refactor sections ask you to go back and change code that you've already written to make improvements.

As you work on the **Your Turn** and **Refactor** sections, you probably won't know what to do at first. You might have to try a few different things before you're successful. That's a normal part of programming. And if you can't figure out some challenges, no worries! There is a code guide at the end of every chapter to check your work.

Check Your Work

At the end of each chapter you will test your code by running it. **Check Your Work** sections have a screenshot of what your game window should look like when your code runs and snippets of what your code should look like.

Grace's Corner

Admiral Grace Hopper was a famous computer scientist. She invented early computing tools and paved the way for programming languages that were closer to English than "machine language." One issue was that moths got into her machine and caused problems. And so she popularized the use of the word *bug* for an error in a program. *Debugging* is the process of finding and fixing errors in your code. When you get stuck, look for debugging help from Admiral Hopper in Grace's Corner boxes.

Ideas for Programmers

These boxes highlight ideas that are important to programming and computer science no matter what language you use to code or what type of programs you want to create.

WHAT IS PYTHON?

Python is a professional programming language. **Programming languages** allow people to give directions to computers.

Who uses Python?

Game Designers • **Data Scientists** • **Quality Assurance Engineers**
Software Engineers • **Scientific Researchers** • **Web Developers**

What are some things that use Python?

Google • Tools for **cancer research** • **Spotify** • **Reddit** • **YouTube**
Instagram • Games like *EVE Online* and *Battlefield 2*
NASA projects like software for the **Kepler Space Observatory**

How does Python work?

Ever wonder how your computer can understand the directions you give it? Computers process all information using 1s and 0s (**ON** and **OFF** switches). We call this **binary**. Yes! Everything you do with your phone, tablet, or computer had to be converted to 1s and 0s for your computer to figure out what to do.

English and other spoken languages are too nonspecific for computers, and binary instructions are too impractical for humans, so we use programming languages to meet in the middle.

Programming languages let us express code in ways we can more easily understand, but they can also be translated to binary instructions that the computer can understand.

Hardware

LOW LEVEL

Machine Code

Compiler ‹ OR › **Interpreter**

A **compiler** translates all programming into machine code in a single session.

Python

An **interpreter** translates programming into machine code one command at a time. Python uses an interpreter.

HIGH LEVEL

Python is a high-level language, so it needs to go through a few layers of translation to get to those 1s and 0s.

English

Installing Python

To build our game, we first have to install Python onto our computer. In addition to everything that Python can do on its own, Python has libraries that allow you to build specific types of programs. Since we are building a game, we will also need to install a library called Pygame.

Why Do We Have to Install Python?

When you download Python, you are actually downloading an interpreter. Programs are just files that contain code that are stored on your computer. To run those files, you need the interpreter. Remember, for program files to run, they have to give instructions to your computer. The interpreter that you download allows the computer to complete the translation from Python all the way to binary.

Interpreter

You may have done programming before by signing into an account and working in a web application in your browser. **Scratch** is a popular first language that is often used this way. You can write real code in a web app, but you can't write a program that can give directions to your computer. You can only affect the web application.

Steps to Install Python

1. Go to **python.org** (or search for **Python Software Foundation**).

2. Find the **Downloads** section at the bottom of the page.

Power Up: Malware, keep out! Only download Python from a trusted source. Make sure that you are on the official Python Software Foundation site.

3. Identify what type of operating system you have. The most common OSs are Windows, Mac OS, and Linux. Click on the name of your OS.

4. Find the download links for the most recent version of Python that starts with a 3. For example: **Python 3.7.0.** Click on the first link to download it.

5. From your downloads, open the installer.

6. In the installer window, if there is a box that says **Add Python to PATH**, make sure it is checked.

7. Click **Install Now.** Wait until you see the message: **Setup was successful!**, then close the installer.

8. You have successfully installed Python!

Operating System

An operating system **(OS)** is a program that manages all the other programs on your computer. This book will cover Windows and Mac OS X. If you have another operating system, take a look at the *Python for Any Device* section on the next page.

A Tale of Two Python Versions

Once upon a time, everyone used Python 2. When Python 3 was released, it made some changes to the way that Python is written. Python 2 stuck around because lots of people still really liked Python 2, and because it's a really big task to change all of your old programs to a new version.

In this book, we will use Python 3 because, starting in 2020, Python 2 won't be updated anymore. Make sure that you download the right version or you may notice that your programs don't work exactly the same way as the examples in this book.

Python for Any Device

To code this game, Python will need to be installed on a computer. However, if you don't have access to a computer or can't download software, you can still learn Python!

Device	Operating System	How to Run Python
Options to Code this Game		
Laptop or Desktop Computer ❯	Windows Mac OS X Linux/UNIX ❯	Download from **python.org** Pip install Pygame
Raspberry Pi ❯	Raspbian ❯	Nothing; Python and Pygame are already installed!
Other Options for Learning Python		
Chromebook ❯	Chrome OS	Use an online Python editor such as: **trinket.io** or **codeanywhere.com**
A school or library computer ❯	any ❯	
Tablet or phone ❯	IOS ❯	Install the app **Python for IOS**
	Android ❯	Install the app **Python3**

The Command Line

Before you can begin to code in Python, you need to learn to use the command line. To launch your game, you need a way to give commands to your operating system. You can do this through the **shell.** The shell is software that runs in a **command line interface.** A command line interface allows you to give commands to the operating system.

To access the command line, we will open a terminal window, also known as a **command prompt.**

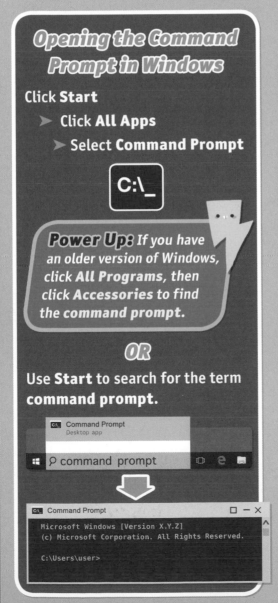

Opening the Command Prompt in Windows

Click **Start**
> Click **All Apps**
> > Select **Command Prompt**

C:_

Power Up: If you have an older version of Windows, click **All Programs**, then click **Accessories** to find the *command prompt.*

OR

Use **Start** to search for the term **command prompt.**

| CA | Command Prompt |
| Desktop app |

🔲 ⌕ command prompt   ⫩ e 📁

CA Command Prompt   🔲 — ✕

Microsoft Windows [Version X.Y.Z]
(c) Microsoft Corporation. All Rights Reserved.

C:\Users\user>

Opening the Terminal in Mac OS

Open the **applications** folder
> Open the **utilities** folder
> > Click on **Terminal**

>_

OR

Use Spotlight to search for the term **terminal.**

Q terminal

TOP HIT
▪ Terminal

● ● ●   ⬆ User — -bash — 80×24
Last login: Fri Jul 13 00:02:52 on console
User— MacBook:~ user$

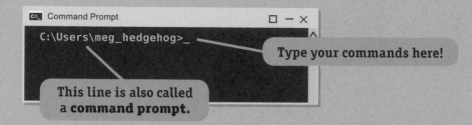

CA   Command Prompt   □ — ✕

C:\Users\meg_hedgehog>_

Type your commands here!

This line is also called
a **command prompt**.

How is using the terminal different from other things I do with my computer?

Think about a car. Many people learn how to drive cars. They can direct the car with the steering wheel, turn on the radio, and check how much gas they have. They are car users. Most people who know how to drive cannot make modifications to the engine to make the car run faster or fix the car when it has broken down, so they take it to a mechanic. Mechanics work under the hood, but drivers use the dashboard.

When you use your computer for school or for fun, you are not programming. You are using other programs. You are a computer user. One of the programs that you use is the operating system, usually Mac OS or Windows. A **command line interface** allows you to give commands to the operating system instead of just using it.

When we use the command line in this book, we are taking our first peeks under the hood and learning to do some simple maintenance, like changing the oil in a car.

Using the Command Line

We can use the command line to navigate around the **directories** and **files** stored on our computers. We can create files, open files, move files, and even delete them, all from the shell.

directory A folder that contains files or other directories. Directories let us organize all the files on our computer.

file A collection of data with a name. This can be a document, picture, video, or program, among other things.

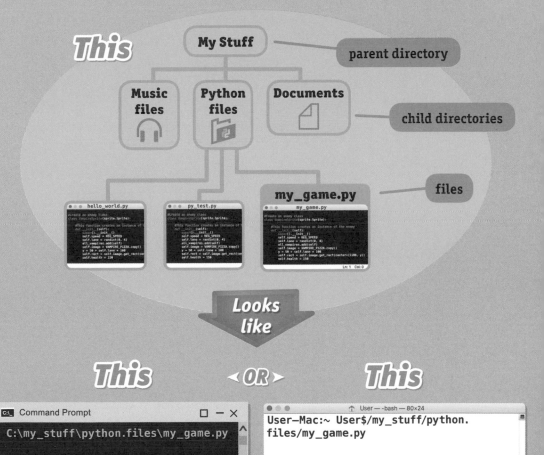

This

My Stuff → parent directory

Music files | Python files | Documents → child directories

hello_world.py | py_test.py | **my_game.py** → files

Looks like

This ‹ OR › This

Command Prompt □ — ✕

C:\my_stuff\python.files\my_game.py

↑ User — -bash — 80×24

User—Mac:~ User$/my_stuff/python.
files/my_game.py

Command Line in the Terminal Window

The first thing that we will do is create a new directory for our Python game files. We'll learn a few basic terminal commands to do this. Follow along with the directions for your operating system.

Mac OS

1. Let's start by taking a look around. Type `ls` (the letter **L** and the letter **S** in lowercase are an abbreviation for the word list) to see what directories are already in your starting directory.

```
● ● ●          ⬆ User — -bash — 80×24
User—Mac:~ User$ ls
Applications   Documents   Library   Music   Desktop
Downloads      Movies      Pictures
```

2. Let's create a new directory. Type `mkdir my_directory` to create a new directory called **my_directory**.

```
● ● ●          ⬆ User — -bash — 80×24
User—Mac:~ User$ mkdir my_directory
```

3. Take a look. Type `ls` again and find **my_directory** in the list on the right side. Here's an example of what a directory list might look like.

```
● ● ●          ⬆ User — -bash — 80×24
User—Mac:~ User$ ls
Applications   Documents   Library    Music   Desktop
Downloads      Movies      Pictures   my_directory ◀
```

4. Now change the name of the directory to **vampire_pizza_directory** by typing `mv my_directory vampire_pizza_directory`. Notice the name of the directory reminds us of what is stored in it.

```
● ● ●          ⬆ User — -bash — 80×24
User—Mac:~ User$ mv my_directory vampire_pizza_directory
```

Use `ls` to check that the directory has been renamed.

5. We can go into the directory using `cd` followed by the name of your new directory. There won't be anything in it yet. When you're done, if you want to go back out of your new directory, you can use `cd ..` (Notice the space between the **d** and the first period.)

6. You've done it! See for yourself. Go into the files app on your computer. Click **user** and any other parent directories until you find the new directory that you created.

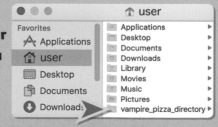

Power Up: *Notice that I'm using the underscore symbol ▮ instead of spaces in my file names. Putting spaces in your file names can cause problems with managing them in the shell. Do not use any spaces in your file names.*

Windows

1. Let's start by taking a look around. Type `dir` to see what directories are already in your starting directory.

```
C:\Users\user>dir
Directory of C:\Users\user
08/02/2019 03:30 PM <DIR>    Desktop
08/02/2019 03:30 PM <DIR>    Documents
08/02/2019 03:30 PM <DIR>    Downloads
08/02/2019 03:30 PM <DIR>    Music
```

2. Let's create a new directory. Type `mkdir my_directory` to create a new directory called **my_directory**.

```
C:\Users\user>mkdir my_directory
```

3. Take a look. Type `dir` again and find **my_directory** in the list on the right side. Here's an example of what a directory list might look like.

```
C:\Users\user>dir
Directory of C:\Users\user
08/02/2019 03:30 PM <DIR>    Desktop
08/02/2019 03:30 PM <DIR>    Documents
08/02/2019 03:30 PM <DIR>    Downloads
08/02/2019 03:30 PM <DIR>    Music
08/02/2019 03:30 PM <DIR>    my_directory
```

4. Now change the name of the directory to **vampire_pizza_directory** by typing: `rename my_directory vampire_pizza_directory`. Notice the name of our directory reminds us of what is stored in it.

```
C:\Users\user>rename my_directory vampire_pizza_directory
```

Use `dir` to check that the directory has been renamed.

5. We can go into the directory using `cd` followed by the name of your new directory. There won't be anything in it yet. (You can check with `dir`.) When you're done if you want to go back out of your new directory, you can use `cd..` (Notice there are no spaces.)

6. You've done it! See for yourself. Go into the files app on your computer. Click **C:** and any other parent directories until you find the new directory that you created.

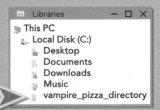

Terminal Command Cheat Sheet

	Command	Action	Examples
Mac	mkdir	Create a new directory	mkdir my_folder
Win	mkdir or md		
Mac	mv	Rename a file or directory	mv my_folder game_folder mv file1.py hello_world.py
Win	rename or ren		rename my_folder game_folder rename file1.py hello_world.py
Mac	ls	List directories and files inside current directory	ls
Win	dir		dir
Mac	cd and cd ..	Change to a new directory	cd game_folder (to change to a specific directory) cd .. (to go back one directory in the pathway)
Win	cd and cd..		cd game_folder (to change to a specific directory) cd.. (to go back one directory in the pathway)
Mac	pwd	Displays the full pathway to your location in the file system	pwd
Win	chdir		chdir
Mac	less	Displays the contents of a file	less hello_world.py
Win	more		more hello_world.py
Mac	exit	Exits the shell and closes the terminal window	exit
Win	exit		exit

The Python Interpreter

When we type **python** in the command line, it runs the Python interpreter. We can do two things:

1. Run Python files, and **2.** Open the **REPL**.

We don't have any Python files yet, so we'll start with the **REPL**.

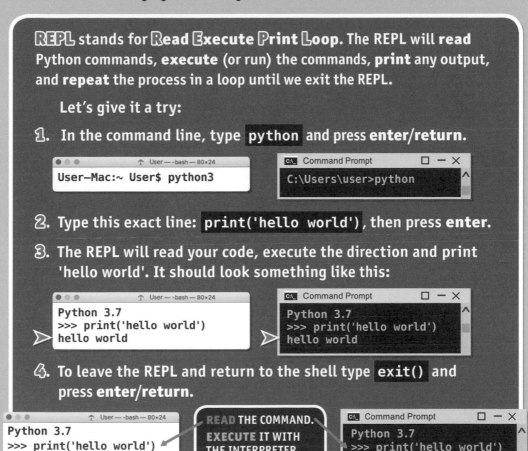

REPL stands for Read Execute Print Loop. The REPL will **read** Python commands, **execute** (or run) the commands, **print** any output, and **repeat** the process in a loop until we exit the REPL.

Let's give it a try:

1. In the command line, type `python` and press **enter/return**.

```
● ● ●            ⬆ User — -bash — 80×24
User–Mac:~ User$ python3
```

```
C:\ Command Prompt          □ — ✕
C:\Users\user>python
```

2. Type this exact line: `print('hello world')`, then press **enter**.

3. The REPL will read your code, execute the direction and print 'hello world'. It should look something like this:

```
● ● ●            ⬆ User — -bash — 80×24
Python 3.7
>>> print('hello world')
hello world
```

```
C:\ Command Prompt          □ — ✕
Python 3.7
>>> print('hello world')
hello world
```

4. To leave the REPL and return to the shell type `exit()` and press **enter/return**.

```
● ● ●            ⬆ User — -bash — 80×24
Python 3.7
>>> print('hello world')
hello world
>>> exit()
User–Mac:~ User$
```

READ THE COMMAND.
EXECUTE IT WITH THE INTERPRETER.
PRINT ANY OUTPUT.
↻ REPEAT IN A LOOP UNTIL YOU EXIT.

```
C:\ Command Prompt          □ — ✕
Python 3.7
>>> print('hello world')
hello world
>>> exit()
C:\Users\user_
```

The **REPL** may look the same as the command line, but you are actually in a new program.

Power Up: *Make sure you are running Python 3. You may need to type* `python3` *to be certain.*

You can tell which program you are in by what is around the area where you are typing:

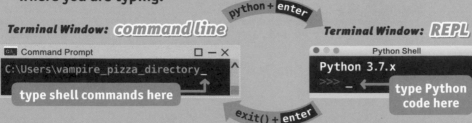

Terminal Window: *command line*

Command Prompt

C:\Users\vampire_pizza_directory_

type shell commands here

python + enter

exit() + enter

Terminal Window: *REPL*

Python Shell

Python 3.7.x

>>>

type Python code here

You can go between the programs by typing `python` to enter the **REPL** and typing `exit()` to return to the command line. These programs do not save anything. Once you exit the **REPL** or close the terminal window, your code goes away. You will learn how to save code in a file later on.

Grace's Corner

Verify that you have installed Python correctly. You can use the REPL to verify your Python installation and check the version.

When you type `python` in the command line and press enter, you should see one of two messages:

If Python is installed correctly, you will see a message with the version number `Python 3.x.x`. Check that the first number is a 3. If it's not, go back to page 10 and follow the steps to install Python 3.

If you are on the wrong pathway or Python is not installed, you will see this message:

"'Python' is not recognized as an internal or external command, operable program or batch file."

If you get this message, try troubleshooting.

1. Check your pathway. Are you in the correct directory?

2. If you don't know where Python is on your computer, go to the start menu in Windows or the application icon in Mac OS and search for **python.exe**.

3. If everything else looks right, but you are still getting the error message, try uninstalling and reinstalling Python.

Play with Python!

We've talked a lot about Python. Let's write some code! You can use this section to learn the basics before you jump into creating your game. You will will practice the basics in **REPL**, which works like this:

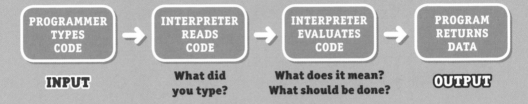

PROGRAMMER TYPES CODE	→	INTERPRETER READS CODE	→	INTERPRETER EVALUATES CODE	→	PROGRAM RETURNS DATA
INPUT		What did you type?		What does it mean? What should be done?		**OUTPUT**

Python Is Good at Math

Did you know that Python can do basic math for you? Python reads the line of code that you wrote, decides what it means or evaluates the code, and then returns an output.

If you type a number and press **enter/return**, it returns the number.

```
Python Shell
Python 3.7.x (v3.7.x, date, time)
>>> 7
7
```

If you type an addition problem, it evaluates the problem and returns the answer.

```
Python Shell
Python 3.7.x (v3.7.x, date, time)
>>> 7 + 7
14
```

You can subtract and multiply, too. Multiply with the asterisk ✱ symbol instead of a times x symbol.

```
Python Shell
Python 3.7.x (v3.7.x, date, time)
>>> 5 - 5
0
>>> 2 * 2
4
```

 **Your Turn**

Type at least five different addition, subtraction, and multiplication problems.

What about Division?

You can divide with Python, too. Just know that it will work a little bit differently than you are used to. You can do floor division with two backslashes. This will give you just a whole number and cut off a remainder.

For example, $10 \div 4 = 2.5$

But if we use floor division, it just drops the remainder .5.

In programming, the numbers that we use are types of data that we are inputting into the program. We call whole numbers **integers**. Numbers with decimals are called **floats**. These are two types of data that we can use when we program.

```
● ● ●              Python Shell
Python 3.7.x (v3.7.x, date, time)
>>> 10 // 4
2
```

You can also do what you think of as true division with one backslash.

```
● ● ●              Python Shell
Python 3.7.x (v3.7.x, date, time)
>>> 1 / 3
0.333333333333333
```

This is usually okay, but you will run into problems with accuracy. To keep things simple, try to use floor division with integers whenever possible.

Thanks for the homework help, Python!

Grace's Corner

You may start to get error messages. Here's one that I got when I was doing some math the other day:

```
● ● ●              Python Shell
Python 3.7.x (v3.7.x, date, time)
>>> 1 = 2
File <stdin>, line 1
SyntaxError: can't assign to literal
```

I went back and saw that I typed an equal sign when I meant to type a plus sign.
In the REPL, you can just try again on the next line.

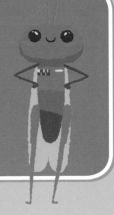

```
                    Python Shell
Python 3.7.x (v3.7.x, date, time)
>>> 1 = 2
File <stdin>, line 1
SyntaxError: can't assign to literal
>>> 1 + 2
3
```

First Words with Python

We've already discovered that we can have the program print words. Actually, it will print anything that we surround with single or double quotes. We call these **strings**. Strings are another type of data that we can use in our programs, just like integers and floats.

Try printing your name.

```
                    Python Shell
Python 3.7.x (v3.7.x, date, time)
>>> print('Meg Hedgehog')
Meg Hedgehog
```

Try printing your favorite song lyrics.

Do you want the lyrics to print on two lines?
Use an \n where you want a line break to appear.

```
                    Python Shell
Python 3.7.x (v3.7.x, date, time)
>>> print('Happy birthday to you \n Happy birthday to you')
Happy birthday to you
 Happy birthday to you
```

 **Your Turn**

Get some practice. Type at least five print statements with different strings. Try writing a poem or listing your favorite foods.

What if you want to use an apostrophe?

Python can't tell the difference between a single quote and an apostrophe, so we have to indicate that it is different by putting an escape character before the apostrophe `\`. The escape character `\` tells the program that the apostrophe is meant to be part of the string and is not ending the string.

```
Python Shell

Python 3.7.x (v3.7.x, date, time)
>>> print('I\'m going over to my friend\'s house today')
I'm going over to my friend's house today
```

Python does not read or understand what is inside single or double quotes in a string. When it evaluates a print statement, it will just print exactly what's in the string.

```
Python Shell

Python 3.7.x (v3.7.x, date, time)
>>> print(3 + 3)
6
>>> print('3 + 3')
3 + 3
```

The second addition problem was surrounded by quotes, so Python didn't bother to find the answer or even to read the problem. It just prints exactly what's inside the quotes.

Grace's Corner

You may find that you are getting more error messages now. Look for some of these common bugs.

`print('oranges'` - missing parenthesis

`print(apples')` - missing quote

`Print('grapes')` - capitalized the print command

`prnt('bananas')` - misspelled the print command

Variables

Variables are used to store information. We often use variables when we want to use data over and over or when we want to use data that will change.

So I could type `12` and get `12` back.

```
●●●          Python Shell
>>> 12
12
```

I could also store **12** in a variable called **age**.

Now if I type `age`, I get `12` back.

```
●●●          Python Shell
>>> age = 12
>>> age
12
```

Think of a variable as a tag for organizing and finding information in your program.

When you create a tag for data in your program, it is called **assigning a variable.**

Variables always follow the same pattern.

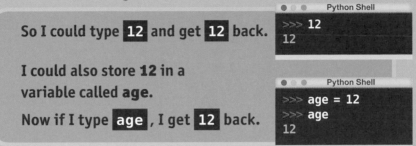

variable name

age = 12

equal sign assigns the name to the data

variable value (data to be stored)

Let's create some variables to see how they work.

```
●●●          Python Shell
>>> temp = 75
>>> weather = 'sunny'
>>> temp
75
>>> weather
sunny
```

Variable names point to objects that have a type and a value.

name = object

age →

TYPE	VALUE
integer	12

age

Here our variable name tag is attached to an integer object with the value 12.

A variable can only store one type of data. For example, it cannot store an integer and a string together. A variable can also store lists of data called **arrays**.

my_cats

The value of a variable can change. It throws out the old value and changes to the value that you most recently typed.

cat_name
'shadow'

```
Python Shell
>>> cat_name = 'shadow'
>>> cat_name = 'smokey'
smokey
```

'shadow'   'smokey'   cat_name

Like in math, code has an **order of operations**. First, it returns the value of anything to the right of the equals sign. Then it assigns the value. Let's look at a couple of examples.

Type `my_answer = 3 + 3`.

What do you think you will get back when you press **enter/return**?

$$my\_answer = \underbrace{3 + 3}_{6}$$
$$my\_answer = 6$$

```
Python Shell
>>> my_answer = 3 + 3
>>> my_answer
6
```

6   my_answer

What about the value of `best_food = string.upper()`?

```
Python Shell
>>> string = 'tacos'
#upper turns all the letters in a string to upper case
>>> best_food = string.upper()
>>> best_food
TACOS
```

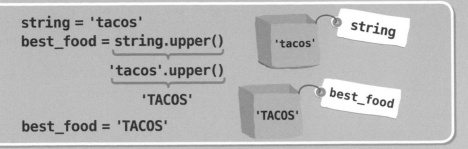

```
string = 'tacos'
best_food = string.upper()
```

```
'tacos'.upper()
```

```
'TACOS'
```

```
best_food = 'TACOS'
```

Can I name a variable anything that I want?

Yes, as long as you follow the naming rules.
You can store the string `'green'`
in a variable labeled `red`:

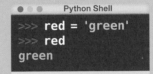

```
>>> red = 'green'
>>> red
green
```

`red = 'green'`.

Every time you type `red` in your program, you would get `green`.

That sounds like fun, but it can get very confusing when you need to keep track of many variables in one program. You should try to pick names that will help you remember what data the variable is storing.

So you might choose something like this:
`background_color = 'green'`.

What are the rules for naming variables?

Don't start with a number.

This: `three_pigs = ['Melvin', 'Delvin', 'Steve']`
Not this: `3_pigs = ['Melvin', 'Delvin', 'Steve']`

Don't include spaces. (Programmers tend to use underscores `_` where they would put a space.)

This: `my_pets = ['cat', 'turtle', 'fish']`
Not this: `my pets = ['cat', 'turtle', 'fish']`

Don't use special words or characters that have a specific meaning in Python.

For example, **+**, **=**, and **#** can never be in a variable name
For example: **class**, **global**, and **import** cannot be variable names

Here are a few tips to make your code look professional:

Use all lowercase letters.

Separate words with underscores.

Choose names that are meaningful and descriptive.

Get Some Input

As the programmer, you can have Python print something that you type using `print()`, but what if you want to print what someone else, like a user, types? For example, in some games you can create your own character name and that name appears on the screen. The game developer didn't pick that name; you (the player) did.

Let's try it. In the **REPL**, type the following:

```
>>> character = input('Enter the name of a character ')
```

When you press **enter/return**, you will see this on the screen:

```
>>> character = input('Enter the name of a character ')
Enter the name of a character _
```

Go ahead and just type in a character name. I'll use **Hedgie the Heroic Hedgehog**.

When you press **enter/return**, you won't see anything new on the screen, but something did happen. Python took the character name you typed and stored it in the variable character.

```
>>> character = input('Enter the name of a character ')
Enter the name of a character Hedgie the Heroic Hedgehog
>>> _
```

So, in my example, Python did this behind the scenes:
character = 'Hedgie the Heroic Hedgehog'

Power Up: You can use a **+** sign to combine a string and a variable that stores a string. This is called **concatination**.

Now type:

```
>>> print('You will be playing ' + character)
```

When I press **enter/return**, I will get this:

```
>>> character = print('Enter the name of a character ')
Enter the name of a character Hedgie the Heroic Hedgehog
>>> print('You will be playing ' + character)
You will be playing Hedgie the Heroic Hedgehog
>>> _
```

Take a Closer Look

```
>>> character = print('Enter the name of a character ')
Enter the name of a character Hedgie the Heroic Hedgehog
>>> print('You will be playing ' + character)
You will be playing Hedgie the Heroic Hedgehog
>>> _
```

```
>>> print('You will be playing ' + character)
```

`'You will be playing '` is a **string** and `character` is a **variable with a value that is a string,** so Python just printed them together. Strings and integers are two different data types, so we can't just combine a string and an integer. If you want to combine them, you can convert the integer to a string using `str()`.

For example, type:

Notice the spaces in `' is '`.

```
>>> age = 317
>>> print(character + ' is ' + str(age))
Hedgie the Heroic Hedgehog is 317
>>> _
```

Your Turn

Try creating a quiz with at least five questions.
Use `input()` to ask questions about a topic that you know a lot about.

Store each question in a different variable.

If you have a friend or family member nearby, you can ask them to fill in the answers. Otherwise, you can fill them in yourself.

When you are done, use `print()` with each variable to show the user's answers.

Grace's Corner

There are many different types of bugs that you might run into when using `input()`.

Here are some things to think about when you get error messages:

Am I trying to combine two different data types when I print?

This: `age = 14`
`print('I am' + str(age) + 'years old')`
Not this: `age = 14`
`print('I am' + age + 'years old')`

Do all parentheses and quotation marks have pairs?

This: `print('I am' + str(age) + 'years old')`
Not this: `print(I am' + str(age + 'years old')`

When I combined strings, did I separate them with a plus sign?

This: `print('I am' + str(age) + 'years old')`
Not this: `print('I am' str(age) 'years old')`

Could the user have typed something I didn't expect, like leaving the prompt blank or using a string instead of an integer?

Functions

Let's pause and look at a pattern that you might have noticed. We've used two commands that have parentheses after them: `print()` and `input()`. Why do we need those parentheses?

Print and **input** are both **functions**. In Python, built-in functions are preprogrammed commands that take in data, do a specific task, and return a response.

> **function** a programmed command that takes in data, completes a specific task, and returns a response

`input` → `function` → `output`

How Functions Work   `function_name('argument')`

Functions have three parts: the **function name**, the **argument**, and the **parentheses**.

* The **function name** tells the program what action to take.

* The **argument** or **arguments** inside the parentheses provide the data needed to run the function.

* The **parentheses** tell the program to go ahead and **execute**, or run, the function.

Take a look at the diagram. This shows the correct **syntax** of a function.

function name

argument (data needed to execute function)

`print('hello world')`

parentheses say "Execute this function!"

Syntax is the word for how a command is written, including the characters, capitalization, and order. Think of syntax as a pattern that you can use to help you program. If you saw the code `range(1,10)`, you might not know what it does, but you do know that this code executes some sort of task called "range" using the integers **1** and **10** as data. That's a pretty good place to start!

Mad Lib!

Let's put together everything that you have learned so far to create your own fill-in-the-blank silly story! You can make up your own story or use mine.

My name is _____ : I run a _____ shop!
　　　　　　　(user_name)　　　　　　　　　(favorite_food)

But now my shop has been overrun by _____ _____.
　　　　　　　　　　　　　　　　　　　　(monster)　　(favorite_food)

But do not worry; I will stop them with my super _____.
　　　　　　　　　　　　　　　　　　　　　　　　　(-ing verb)

Power Up: Remember the **REPL** doesn't save your code. Stay in the **REPL** until you've completed the whole Mad Lib.

How can we create a program that lets a user fill in the blanks and then read the story with their responses filled in?

Let's break it down into parts. Here are the things that we will need the program to do:

What needs to happen	How we do that with Python
Ask the user to fill in the blanks with words.	For each blank word, use the **input()** function. Create a unique variable for each user response.
Display the story with the new words filled in.	Use **print()** to display the story on the screen. In the print argument, combine strings with variables correctly.

Part 1: Fill in the Blanks

According to our chart, we need to ask the user to fill in the blanks. For example:

```
>>> user_name = input('what is your name?')
what is your name?_
```

```
>>> favorite_food = input('what is favorite food?')
what is your favorite food?_
```

Use this pattern to create a separate line of code for each blank: **user_name**, **favorite_food**, **monster**, and **verb**.

Part 2: Print the New Story

The next step is to print the story with the user's words. You will use the `print()` function. For example:

```
>>> print('My name is ' + user_name)
My name is Meg Hedgehog_
>>> print('I run a ' + favorite_food + ' shop!')
I run a rice pudding shop!_
```

Go ahead and type the story using the variable names that you created. Use a print function for each sentence of the story. Press **enter/return** to read the silly story.

Part 3: Debugging

It is nearly impossible for programmers to create a program without any bugs on the first try. So you should expect to get error messages before you complete your program. Your program might display the story in a way that you didn't intend, such as with blank words or missing spaces. This kind of bug is called a **logic error**.

Each time you get an error message, first read the message for clues. If you're stumped, look back at some of the **Grace's Corner** boxes in the last few pages for tips.

Error messages can feel discouraging, but they are a normal part of writing programs. Stick with it and don't forget to congratulate yourself for your persistence and debugging skills when you are done!

Level Up!

0 1 2 3 4 5 6 7 8 9 10 11 12 13 ★

Congratulations! You've finished the tutorial. You have learned three very important concepts: **data types**, **variables**, and **functions**. You will use these concepts to program your game!

For now, let's exit out of the **REPL** so that we can finish setting up for our game. To leave the **REPL** and return to the command line, type **exit()** and press **enter/return**. You should see your file pathway:

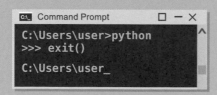

```
Command Prompt          □ — ✕
C:\Users\user>python
>>> exit()

C:\Users\user_
```

```
● ● ●              ⬆ User — -bash — 80×24
User—Mac:~ User$ python3
>>> exit()
User—Mac:~ User$
```

The Development Environment

We can use the REPL to play around with Python, but if we want to create and share programs, like games, we need to use an IDE (integrated development environment) or text editor to create and save program files.

When you installed Python, it came with **IDLE**, a Python IDE, with it. IDLE is made up of a code editor (where you type in your code) and other helpful tools. To write, save, and run programs, you will need two windows open on your screen: your IDE to create and save your programs, and the terminal window to run your programs.

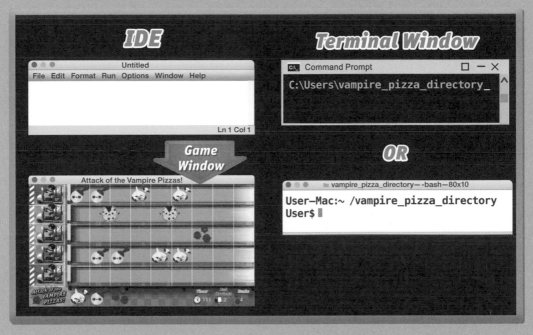

When you run Pygame, it will open up a game window where you can see your program run.

You also have the option to use a different IDE. There are several free options online, such as **Sublime Text** or **Thonny**. If you choose to use a different IDE, you will need to install it separately.

Try it out.

1. Go to your applications folder or type IDLE into the search bar to open up IDLE. If you don't see IDLE, Python may not have installed correctly. Go back to page 10 and try the installation process again.

2. When you open IDLE, you see the Python shell. This is a REPL, just like we used in the terminal. Click **File**, then **New File**, to open a code editor window.

3. Once you've opened a new file, close the Python shell. You won't need it to code your game.

Python Shell

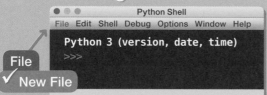

Code Editor

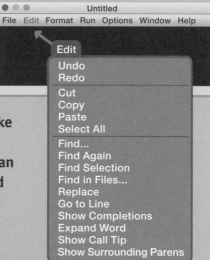

IDLE also has some options that will make coding more efficient. You can select these options from the **Edit** tab or you can use keyboard shortcuts. These keyboard shortcuts will save you lots of time and frustration as you create your game.

Operation	Shortcut	What It Does
Undo	Ctrl + Z	Undo a mistake
Redo	Ctrl + Shift + Z	Bring back something you undid
Cut	Ctrl + X	Cut or copy lines of code and paste them back to another location in your program
Copy	Ctrl + C	
Paste	Ctrl + V	
Find	Ctrl + F	Find words in your program
Replace	Ctrl + H	Change a word in your program
Show Parens	Ctrl + 0	Highlight parentheses in a line of code
Indent	Ctrl +]	Indent a highlighted area by 4 spaces
Dedent	Ctrl + [	Unindent an area by 4 spaces
Comment Out	Alt + 3	Make a highlighted area of code into a comment or vice versa
Uncomment	Alt + 4	

Installing Pygame

We now have Python, the REPL, and IDLE up and running. We are just missing one more thing: Pygame! Pygame is a library of Python. It adds some features to Python that will allow you to do things like create our game display and make and interact with game characters.

Instead of downloading Pygame from the Internet, we are going to do a **pip install.** This command will search an index of Python libraries online, find the one that we are requesting, and download and install it for us.

Steps to Install Pygame

1. Open the terminal window.

2. Windows users type: `python -m pip install -U pygame --user`

Win ▷
```
C:\ Command Prompt                              □ − ×
C:\Users\user>python -m pip install -U pygame --user
```

Mac users may need to type:

`python3 -m pip install -U pygame --user`

Mac ▷
```
●●●            ⬆ User — -bash — 80×24
User—Mac:~ User$ python3 -m pip install -U pygame --user
```

3. Wait. You will see text in the terminal.
   When you see the message **"successfully installed pygame,"** you will know it is finished.

4. Check to see if it worked. Type:

`python —m pygame.examples.aliens`

to run an example program.

Mac users may need to type:

`python3 —m pygame.examples.aliens`

5. If you see the game aliens, it worked! You can move on to the next page. If it didn't work, try the troubleshooting tips.

Troubleshooting

Check that you typed the line exactly as shown. Are the characters, spacing, and capitalization all exactly the same?

Try typing the same line, but type `python3` instead of `python`.

If you have a Mac, try `python3 —m pygame.examples.aliens`.

If you have Windows, try `python —m pygame.examples.aliens`.

If you're still stuck, go to this website:
pygame.org/wiki/GettingStarted

Game Development

Before we dive into developing our game, let's take a minute to think about what makes a game fun to play.

The Elements of Game Design:
What makes the games you play fun?

Space
Where the game takes place
What is the setting? What is the look and feel of the design?

Rules
The boundaries of game play
What is allowed? What is not allowed?

Mechanics
What you do in the game
What actions is the player taking?

Goals
How you win
What do you need to achieve or avoid to win the game?

Components
The game pieces/sprites
What are the different parts of the game, including characters, enemies, and items?

Your Turn

Think about your favorite video game or mobile game. Can you identify each of the five elements of game design for that game?

What Makes a Game Fun?

Game designers carefully develop each of the five elements to create a fun and balanced game.

Interesting themes and stories contribute to a player's enjoyment of games.

Games that have the right amount of challenge and are not too easy or difficult to win are the most fun. We call this balance. Games without any challenge are boring, and games with too much challenge are frustrating. To adjust balance, you can alter one or more of the five elements of game design.

Idea to Game: The Software Development Process

Think about your favorite game again. It wasn't developed on the first try by one person. It likely took a team of developers months or years to create. And the version that you play was not the first version that was created. This is because programming is a **collaborative** and **iterative** process.

A **collaborative process** means people work together to create software. Programs get better when multiple people work on them and test them. You can build the game in this book on your own or with a friend. If you do build it on your own, you should show it to your friends and get their feedback to make it even better.

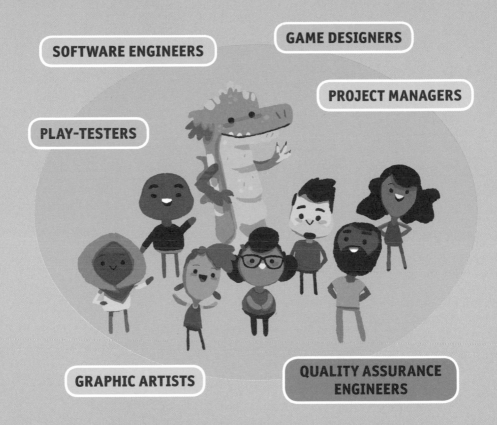

SOFTWARE ENGINEERS

GAME DESIGNERS

PROJECT MANAGERS

PLAY-TESTERS

GRAPHIC ARTISTS

QUALITY ASSURANCE ENGINEERS

An **iterative process** means that software goes through a process to improve it before it is finished. Programmers develop a first draft of their program and then test it. Based on the tests, they iterate to make changes and improvements. Programmers also get feedback from people who will be using their software: users or players. After testing and improving the game several times, programmers have people playtest the game. They ask the play-testers for feedback and make changes to the game based on that feedback.

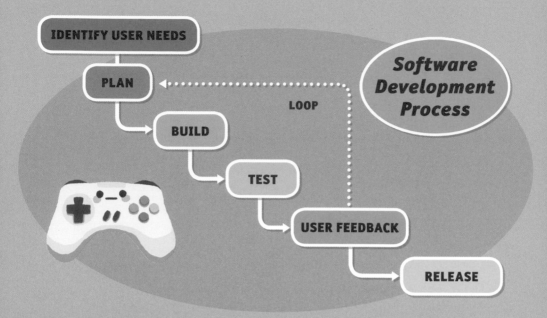

IDENTIFY USER NEEDS

PLAN

LOOP

BUILD

TEST

USER FEEDBACK

RELEASE

Software Development Process

As you create your game, you will have opportunities to iterate on your program.

In each chapter, you will **plan** a game feature, **build** that game feature, and **test** what you built. When you run into bugs, you continue the loop by planning changes, building the changes, and testing the changes. You repeat this loop until the new feature works the way you want it to.

PLAN

BUILD

TEST

Ideas for Programmers

Who Is My User?

A **user** is a person who will use the program you are developing after it is complete. For example, you are the user of every app you have downloaded. When we create games, our users are the people who will play the game for fun: the **players**. Game developers start the development process by asking questions like: Who will play my game? What will my players enjoy? What do my players need to know to play my game? Is there anything that will get in the way of my players understanding or enjoying the game?

Planning with the user or player in mind is called **user-centered design**.

Problem-Solving & Debugging

As you program your game, you will run into problems that you won't know how to solve right away and bugs that will take some time to fix. Your role as a game designer is not just to write code; it's also to figure out what code will create the game that you want and to fix the code when something goes wrong. Your role is to be a problem-solver.

You may have to try different solutions. You may need to try many times. With perseverance, you can figure it out! When this happens, you won't be alone. Look for the **Power Up** and **Grace's Corner** boxes for help. You can also get help from your new community. . . .

Welcome to the Python Community

There is a global community of programmers who use Python. Some are professional programmers, some program for fun, and some are just learning Python like you are. You can also be part of this community.

Finding Help and Inspiration Online

On websites like Pygame.org, you can share your games and see the games that others have created. Python is an open-source language. That means anyone is free to use it and anyone is free to add on to it or improve it.

You can also look for help when you get stuck. If you'd like to ask for help, follow these steps:

1. Look for the answer online in documentation and forums first. Usually, you will find what you need! Only post questions that you can't find an answer to somewhere else.

2. Don't expect others to solve your problem. They should only guide you in the right direction. Ask how a specific concept works, but don't copy and paste in code and ask why it isn't working.

3. Include important information: You are using **Python 3**. Describe what you did to try to debug and what the outcome was.

Here are some beginner-friendly places to start:

wiki.python.org
python.org/wiki
raspberrypi.org/forums

Be a good community member

Remember, all online safety guidelines still apply:

✳ Get permission from a parent or guardian and share with them what you are learning

✳ Don't give out your full name or any personal information

✳ Don't feed the trolls (aka don't respond to any negative comments)

✳ Tell a trusted adult if someone says something that makes you uncomfortable

It's okay to:

✳ Let people know that you are a student and that you are new to Python

✳ Share the work of others with **attribution** (giving credit)

✳ Share your own work

Using Documentation and Tutorials

There's lots of information online about Python. Information about what different functions do and how to use them is called **documentation**. Documentation isn't always easy to read, but it can give you some hints about what you can try or where else you can look.

Tutorials are websites and videos made by Python programmers that will guide you through learning Python. There are free Python books online as well as YouTube videos about using most Python functions.

Using Code Snippets

You will find many amazing games that others have created on the Pygame website. If someone created something that you want to use, you probably can.

On Pygame.org, descriptions of the game will also tell you if you are allowed to use the code. If it says it's open to use, you should only take the part of the code you need and modify it to fit your game. A piece of code from a larger program is referred to as a **code snippet**. If you do use a code snippet, you should always give attribution, or mention the original programmer. You can do this by creating a comment above the code you used in your program. If you use a significant amount of someone else's code, you should also give attribution in the description of your game anywhere that you post it. For example, you could say, "*Scoring system based on [game name with link].*"

Creating Comments

1. Start a new line of code anywhere in your program.

2. Type the hash **#** symbol. This character tells Python to ignore whatever comes after it. Comments are for people to read, not for the program.

3. Type whatever you like after the hash # character.

If you're commenting to give attribution, place the comment directly above the code snippet you used. Include who wrote the code and where you got it from.

You can also use comments for other purposes:

Explain what a code snippet does, either to remind yourself or to let other programmers know.

Add a reminder for yourself if you want to go back and change or add something later.

Explain why you wrote your code the way that you did if there is more than one way to do it.

Label sections to stay organized.

You can also add a hash # character in front of a line of code to temporarily take it out of your program. This is called **commenting out the code.** It is a strategy used to help programmers find a line of code with a bug.

You have installed Python and Pygame. You have learned how to use the shell and REPL. You've written a simple Python program. You've learned how games are developed and how to find resources online. You've already completed some of the hardest parts of learning to program.

You are now ready to *Code This Game*!

How to Read the Code

In the instruction section of each chapter, we will use a **diff format** to guide you in creating your game. This is a format that shows the differences between your file **before** adding new code and your file **after** adding new code. Let's look at how to read a diff:

>>> **Type This**

```
#Asks for the user's name and assigns it to a variable called name
name = input('What is your name?')
print('Hello world')
#Prints a greeting for the user
print('Hello, ' + name)

#To Do: Ask for the user's favorite animal here
#To Do: Add the print statement with fav_animal here
```

➕ Code that is shaded in green needs to be added to your program.

This is what the code should look like after a change.

➖ Code that is shaded in red needs to be removed or changed.

You don't always need to delete the whole line. You may be able to make a change without retyping the entire line.

❗ Comments shaded in purple are "to dos" for you.

Look for directions in the text that tell you how to add the code. You do not need to type these comments. Instead, add the new code where the "To Do" comment indicates.

#Comments in the diffs explain what the code does.

They are important to read so that you understand the code you are writing and can try it on your own later. You do not need to type these comments in your own program.

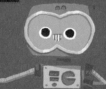

Part 2
Code This Game

Chapter 1
Set Up the Game Window

Imagining Your Game

You are going to program a video game called *Attack of the Vampire Pizzas!* Programs, including games, are made up of many parts that work together. It is important to first think through the game and how you want it to work. After you understand the game as a whole, we will break it down into parts and work on one part at a time. This is called **decomposition** and is a skill that game designers and software engineers use on a daily basis. Let's take a look at the game that you are about to build!

Game Elements in Attack of the Vampire Pizzas!

You have just opened a new pizza restaurant. **Congratulations!** Unfortunately, your pizza place has been infiltrated by **vampire pizzas!** Customers who get vampire pizzas are very unhappy because they drink all the pizza sauce. Those customers leave bad reviews on your pizza-delivery app. If you get three bad reviews, your restaurant won't get enough customers and will need to close down. If you can destroy the vampire pizzas before customers see them, you will only receive good reviews for your yummy pizza!

The **goal** of the game is to prevent vampire pizzas from reaching the pizza boxes at the end of your assembly line. If the player can survive for three minutes without having three or more vampire pizzas reach the boxes, then the player wins. If three vampire pizzas reach the delivery boxes before the three minutes is up, then the player loses the game.

The player can set different kinds of traps to stop the vampire pizzas from reaching the delivery boxes. Players can purchase traps with pizza bucks, which they earn over time. The wooden pizza cutter does damage to the vampire pizzas. The garlic slows down the vampire pizzas. Pepperoni helps the player earn pizza bucks faster. The vampire pizzas and the traps are game **components**. The main **mechanics** of the game are purchasing and setting traps.

Our game will take place on a single screen made up of a grid. Each row of the grid is an assembly line that ends in pizza delivery boxes on a moped. The vampire pizzas will travel along a row toward a pizza delivery box. This is the space where the game takes place. Each trap costs a set amount of pizza bucks. Only one trap is allowed on each tile, and players must select and set one trap at a time. These are some of the rules of the game.

Now that you know how the game works, we can think about the different parts of the game that we will need to build.

Background grid

Vampire pizzas

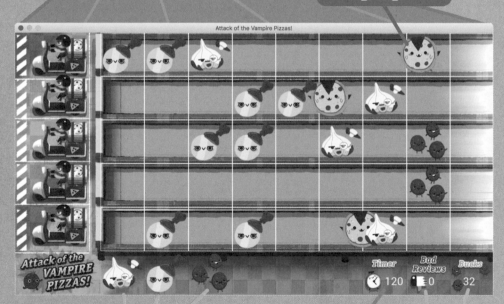

Three kinds of traps

Game timer

Score trackers

Each of these parts will need to be broken down into even smaller subparts. Let's look at an example:

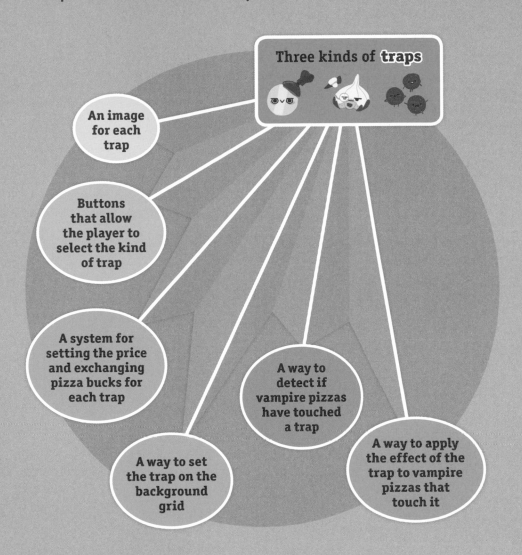

As you can see, even a game that seems simple can be complex to build. In this tutorial, I will guide you through the development process as you build each part of the game. As you code this game, you will probably get stuck many times. That is because you are doing a very complex task. When you get stuck, the important thing is to keep going!

Structure of a Pygame Program

Pygame programs are broken up into two parts: the **game setup** and the **game loop.**

The game setup will be at the top of our program. In the game setup, we will include the elements shown in the diagram from top to bottom.

The game setup runs once when we first launch our program file. Then the game loop section runs until we quit playing.

Game Setup

1. Import libraries
2. Initialize Pygame
3. Create a game window
4. Create global constants
5. Load assets
6. Create game objects
7. Initialize game objects

The game loop repeats over and over as we play the game until we exit. In the game loop, we will include the elements shown in the diagram from top to bottom.

In this chapter, we are going to set up the structure of our program. As you work through the book, you can refer back to this diagram to keep your game organized.

Game Loop

 RUN   *or*   EXIT

1. Listen for and handle events
2. Spawn sprites
3. Update game objects
4. Draw all surfaces
5. Display all surfaces
6. Repeat until the loop is broken (the player wins the game, loses the game, or quits)

1. Optional: Post-Game Loop
2. Clean Up/Close Game

Create a Program File

To begin, we will create a new file for our program.

Through the Code Editor

1. Open **IDLE**.

2. Create a new file by selecting **File → New File**.

3. Save your file by selecting **File → Save**.

   ○ Find and open **vampire_pizza_directory**.

   ○ Name the file **VampirePizzaAttack.py**.

   ○ Check that the file type is a Python file or **.py**.

   ○ Click **Save**.

   ○ Look for the new file name at the top of your code editor window.

4. Close the window labeled **Python Shell**.

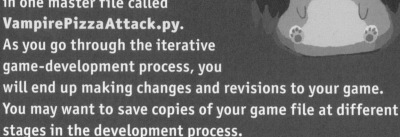

Saving Your Work

In this book, we will work in one master file called **VampirePizzaAttack.py**. As you go through the iterative game-development process, you will end up making changes and revisions to your game. You may want to save copies of your game file at different stages in the development process.

Version control helps you keep track of all of your revisions so that you know you are working in the most up-to-date file and so that if something goes wrong, you can go back to an earlier version of the file if you need to. One way to do this is by using the **Save As** feature to create backup copies of your game. Name the backup files to indicate the phase in the development process, for example, **chap1_backup.py**.

Version-control tools like **Git** or **Bitbucket** help you manage more complex version control.

Now that your program file is named and saved, you should save it often. You can click **ctrl/cmd + s**, or you can use **File → Save**. Program files do not autosave. You must save the program every time that you run the game after making a change to the code. If you forget to save, it will not run your changes.

Power Up: *Complete the activities on pages 21–34 to learn the basics of Python before you start to program your game.*

In this chapter, we will set up the basic structure of our program. This will allow the game to run.

To do this, we need to do four things:

1. Import the Pygame library.

2. Start and stop Pygame.

3. Create a window to play the game in.

4. Set up the game loop.

Import Libraries

Let's start programming!

Take a look at the Pygame program structure. We'll start with game setup. The first thing that we want to do is import the libraries that we need. Remember, libraries extend the abilities of Python. Libraries are also called **packages** or **modules.** We need to import them into our program to gain access to them. Let's import Pygame.

Game Setup

1. **Import any libraries that we need**
2. Initialize Pygame
3. Create a game window
4. Create global constants
5. Load assets
6. Create game objects
7. Initialize game objects

To do this we will use an **import** statement.

>>> **Type This**

```
#Import libraries
import pygame
from pygame import *
```

> # The comment above each line of code explains what that code does. You only need to type the code, not the comments.

Import tells Python to use a certain library in your program. In this case you imported the Pygame library into your program.

The next line tells the program which parts of Pygame we want to import. You imported all of Pygame for this tutorial. When importing a library, the asterisk ***** symbol means "all," or to import the entire library. As you learn to make more complex games, you may want to import only specific parts of Pygame that you need in order to improve the processing speed of the game. We don't need to worry about that for this game.

Initialize Pygame

Next, we need to **initialize** Pygame. This makes the Pygame library do the behind-the-scenes setup it needs in order to run.

> **Initializing** variables or objects prepares them to be used for the first time in a program.

Game Setup

1. Import any libraries that we need
2. **Initialize Pygame**
3. Create a game window
4. Create global constants
5. Load assets
6. Create game objects
7. Initialize game objects

>>> **Type This**

```
#Import libraries
import pygame
from pygame import *
#Initialize pygame
pygame.init()
```

Ideas for Programmers

The Building Blocks of Python

Python is an **object-oriented programming** language. This means that we build the instructions for our program by making statements about **objects**.

Methods complete a task related to an object. **Arguments** are the information that methods need in order to run. We tell objects what to do using methods and how to do it using arguments.

We can use a pattern called **dot notation** to put together statements with these building blocks:

> Objects
> Methods
> Arguments
> Attributes

Object   **Method**   **Argument**

Using a Method in Python

Object . **Method** (**Argument** , **Argument**)

A method is a type of function that is attached to a specific object.

Methods may require arguments.

A function is a programmed command that takes in data, completes a specific task, and returns a response.

Example:

```
pizza.add_toppings(onions, peppers, mushrooms)
```

Object
WHAT is being affected

Method
The ACTION being taken

Arguments
HOW the action will be done

When you initialized Pygame, you used a method **init()** on the object **pygame**. This method did not have any arguments, so the parentheses were empty.

Using an Attribute in Python

Variables that are attached to objects are called **attributes**. We keep information about objects in attributes.

We can also use the dot notation pattern to put together this type of statement:

> **Object** . **Attribute**

Example:

```
pizza.size = 3
large.pie = pizza.size * 2
```

Object	**Attribute**
WHAT the data is about	DATA about an object

Create Window

To create the game window, you will use an object called **display**. We are going to tell the game window to be a certain size using the method `set_mode`.

Game Setup

1. Import any libraries that we need
2. Initialize Pygame
3. **Create a game window**
4. Create global constants
5. Load assets
6. Create game objects
7. Initialize game objects

>>> Type This

```
import pygame
from pygame import *
#Initialize pygame
pygame.init()

#Create window
GAME_WINDOW = display.set_mode((900, 400))
#To Do: Add window caption here
```

Take a Closer Look

This method creates the game window.

```
import pygame
from pygame import *
#Initialize pygame
pygame.init()

#Create window
GAME_WINDOW = display.set_mode((900, 400))
#To Do: Add window caption here
```

```
GAME_WINDOW = display.set_mode((900, 400))
```

Object **Method** **Argument**

The data type of this argument is a **tuple**. Tuples are ordered items that are surrounded by parentheses. This is one argument: **(width, height)**. The whole argument goes in the parentheses after the method.

We need to use another method to add a window caption. Use what you know about how objects, methods, and arguments work together to add this to your code. Add it in the location shown by the ❗ `purple comment` on the previous page.

1. The object is `display`.

2. The method is `set_caption`.

3. The argument is `'Attack of the Vampire Pizzas!'`.

Check Your Work

```
import pygame
from pygame import *
#Initialize pygame
pygame.init()

#Create window
GAME_WINDOW = display.set_mode((900, 400))
display.set_caption('Attack of the Vampire Pizzas!')
```

*Try out every **Your Turn** section, even if you are not sure what to do. All the **Your Turn** challenges need to be completed to build your game. You can check your work after each **Your Turn** challenge or at the end of each chapter. Flip there at any time to see what the code looks like.*

Ideas for Programmers

Loops and Booleans

Loops allow us to run a block of code repeatedly. We use a loop that we'll call the **game loop** to make the game run continuously until we exit. To create the game loop, you need to use a data type called **booleans**.

Booleans

Data is information that we use in our program, and there are different data types we can use. You already know about integers (whole numbers) and strings (any type of character surrounded by quotes). **Booleans** are another type of data, and this data type only has two values: **True** or **False**. We will use booleans, sometimes called **bools** for short, in a **while loop** to create our game loop.

While Loops

There are two types of loops in Python: **while loops** and **for loops.** The loop that runs our game is a while loop. While loops run a block of code over and over while a certain condition is met. We encounter while loops in our everyday lives. For example, you might follow a while loop that goes something like this:

While it is raining out, keep your umbrella open.

If we could make this into Python code, it would look like this:

```
raining = True
while raining:
    umbrella.open()
```

Did you recognize the boolean in this code? The value of raining is **True**. This means that as long as the value of raining is **True**, the loop will run and repeat the function `open`.

If the value of raining gets changed to **False**, then the loop will stop running the function `open` . Raining is a **condition**. You can check if a condition is True (it is raining) or if it is False (it is not raining).

Let's take a closer look at the **syntax** of a while loop. Remember, syntax is the pattern used to create while loops in Python.

While a condition is True   Condition to check   Colon

```
while condition:
    indented code block
```

Indented four spaces   Instructions to be repeated until the loop stops

Indentation Isn't Just for Writing

You may be familiar with indentation from writing. A space before the start of the first sentence signals that you are starting a new paragraph.

In Python, you use indentation to signal which lines of code should be repeated as part of a loop. The first line of the loop, the **while** statement, is written as normal. Anything inside the loop must be indented exactly four spaces. (Later you will learn about other times to use indentation.)

Python is very picky about indentation. If you accidentally use three spaces or five spaces, you will get an error. You can debug the error by adjusting the number of spaces to four. Python is not picky about skipping blank lines, though. Empty lines don't matter at all.

The Game Loop

We need to activate the display in our game loop.

Games use a loop that continuously runs while you are playing. Each time the loop runs through, we call it an **iteration**. This loop runs the code inside it over and over as long as the value of running is True. Take a look at the code and its translation below.

The next line will be inside of the loop so it should be indented four spaces. You will learn more about the code inside of this loop later. For now, type the code exactly as you see it below.

Game Loop

RUN *or* EXIT

1. Listen for and handle events
2. Spawn sprites
3. Update game objects
4. Draw all surfaces
5. Display all surfaces
6. Repeat until the loop is broken (the player wins the game, loses the game, or quits)

1. Optional: Post-Game Loop
2. Clean Up/Close Game

>>> **Type This**

```
GAME_WINDOW = display.set_mode((900, 400))
display.set_caption('Attack of the Vampire Pizzas!')

#-------------------------------------------
#Start Main Game Loop
game_running = True
#Game Loop
while game_running:

#Check for events
    for event in pygame.event.get():

#Exit loop on quit
        if event.type == QUIT:
            game_running = False
    display.update()

#End of main game loop
#-------------------------------------------
#Clean up game
pygame.quit()
```

Take a Closer Look

```
game_running = True
while game_running:
```

While it is true that the game is running, keep repeating the game loop.

As long as game_running = True, this loop will run.

```
game_running = True

while game_running:

    for event in pygame.event.get():

        if event.type == QUIT:

            game_running = False

    display.update()

pygame.quit()
```

Each block shows an indent of 4 spaces.

This is a different kind of loop that is checking for **events** (things that happen in the game) and updating our window to show what happens.

If the game ends or the player quits, the value of **game_running** is changed to **False** and the loop will exit after this iteration (because **game_running** no longer = True).

Ideas for Programmers

Control Structures

You may have noticed that your code runs in order from the top of the program file to the bottom. We need our programs to do more complex things than follow directions in order, like repeat instructions with a loop or only run some instructions if certain conditions are met. An example of this is stopping the game loop only if the player quits the game. Loops and if statements are examples of **control structures** that let us control the flow of our program. Take a look at the flow of the code that we just wrote:

```python
game_running = True
while game_running:
    for event in pygame.event.get():
        if event.type == QUIT:
            game_running = False
        display.update()
pygame.quit()
```

First: We assign the value **True** to running.

Next: The game loop runs until the value of running is changed to **False**.

Last: The **quit()** function will only run after the game loop stops running. The game window will close.

Refactor

When you first write a program, it's like writing the rough draft of a story or an essay. You will end up revising it several times before the final version of the game is done.

Programmers regularly clean up, revise, and reorder their code. This is called refactoring. We will refactor as we build the game.

Why do we need to refactor?

There are several reasons to refactor:

Organize Your Game

You may want to adjust the code to better fit the game structure.

Make Your Code More Efficient or Useful

For example, you might be able to use a short loop instead of a long block of code, or you might want to create a variable that you can easily change later on.

Make Your Code More Readable

You can make your code easier to read by taking out or creating empty lines, changing confusing variable names, or adding in comments that describe what parts of the code do.

Make Your Code Work with New Features

Games have lots of different parts. When you add a new part, like enemies, you may have to adjust how the existing code works, like making changes to the player characters so that they can interact with the new enemies.

It will be easier to make changes later on if we store the length and width values in variables.

Power Up: If you need to move code around your program, you can use **cut (ctrl/cmd + x)** and **paste (ctrl/cmd + v)** instead of re-typing.

```
import pygame
from pygame import *

#Initialize pygame
pygame.init()

#Define constant variables
#To Do: Create a variable for the window width here
#To Do: Create a variable for the window height here
#To Do: Create a variable for window resolution here

#Create window
#To Do: Replace the argument in the set_mode method below
GAME_WINDOW = display.set_mode((900, 400))

display.set_caption('Attack of the Vampire Pizzas!')
```

1. Go back to the code you used to set up the game window. Assign the values **900** and **400** to variables named `WINDOW_WIDTH` and `WINDOW_HEIGHT`.

2. Create a third variable called `WINDOW_RES`. This is short for **window resolution**. Set the value of `WINDOW_RES` equal to `(WINDOW_WIDTH, WINDOW_HEIGHT)`. Now you can use the variables separately or as a set.

3. Now replace `(900, 400)` with the variable `WINDOW_RES` as an argument in the `display.set_mode()` function.

You can check your progress at the end of the chapter. Be sure to check if you need to rearrange any of your code.

Test It Out

It is important to test your game often as you build it. When you see this symbol, you'll know that it is a good time to test out what you've done so far.

Running a Python File

To test your game, you will need to run the Python file. Follow the steps below:

1. Save your file. You can press **ctrl/cmd + s** on the keyboard or you can select **File ➔ Save** in the text editor.

2. Open the **terminal window** and go to the directory where you have stored the file. You can use:
   `cd vampire_pizza_directory`

3. Type `python VampirePizzaAttack.py`

4. Press **enter/return**.

One of three things will happen:

❋ You will see an empty Pygame window open on your screen, and it will stay open until you close it.

❋ You will see an empty Pygame window open and then close quickly on your screen.

❋ You will get an error message in the terminal window.

If you get an error message related to your directory or file, try the following strategies:

❋ Read the error message to see if it gives you any hints, like pointing to part of the command.

❋ Check your file path using **dir** or check the files system in your OS.

❋ Go to page 18 to review shell commands and tips.

If you get an error message related to your Python code or the window closes on its own, you need to debug your code. Take a look at **Grace's Corner** on the next page for tips.

If everything works correctly, you will see a Pygame window that stays open. It will look like this: ➡

> Attack of the Vampire Pizzas!

Grace's Corner

If you need to debug your program, try the following strategies:

1. Read the error message for clues. Does it give you a line number or any words that you recognize?

2. Use the code on the next page and compare it line by line, character by character, with your own.

3. Indentation is tricky. Try retyping the game loop, paying special attention to how many times you press the space bar for each line.

To run your file again after debugging:

❀ Close the game window.

❀ Save the changes in the IDLE code file `cmd` / `ctrl` + `s`.

❀ In the terminal window, press `↑` + `enter` to run the same file again.

Level Up!

0 1 2 3 4 5 6 7 8 9 10 11 12 13 ★

Congratulations! You made the game window appear. You have already started to program your first Python game!

```python
#Set up game

#Import libraries
import pygame
from pygame import *

#Initialize Pygame
pygame.init()

#--------------------------------------------
#Define constant variables

#Define the parameters of the game window
WINDOW_WIDTH = 900
WINDOW_HEIGHT = 400
WINDOW_RES = (WINDOW_WIDTH, WINDOW_HEIGHT)


#--------------------------------------------
#Load assets

#Create window
GAME_WINDOW = display.set_mode(WINDOW_RES)
display.set_caption('Attack of the Vampire Pizzas!')


#--------------------------------------------
#Start main game loop

#Game loop
game_running = True
while game_running:


#--------------------------------------------
#Check for events

    #Checking for and handling events
    for event in pygame.event.get():

        #Exit loop on quit
        if event.type == QUIT:
            game_running = False

#--------------------------------------------
#Update display.
    display.update()

#Close main game loop
#--------------------------------------------

#Clean up game
pygame.quit()
```

Chapter 2
Adding Assets

In this chapter, you will learn to:

1. Load images into your program.

2. Create Pygame surfaces.

3. Display images in your game window.

You can add images to your game! We call these images **assets**.

Assets are images, videos, or other media that are not code that will be part of your game.

How Does Graphics Programming Work?

Programming graphics works differently than drawing graphics. **Graphics programming** creates the impression that an image is moving, but in reality the computer is redrawing an image at a new location and erasing the image at the old location. When this happens at the speed that computers can process, it appears that graphics are moving smoothly across the screen.

You might have seen an effect like this in flipbooks. Each page shows a slightly different image. When you flip the pages quickly, the images blur together to create the illusion of movement:

In computer animation, a similar concept is used called **buffering**. A **buffer** is like a page in the flipbook. Pygame uses **double buffering**, so there are two buffers, or "pages," that are active at once in our flipbook. The buffers are actually blocks of memory. The program "flips" through the buffers. The screen displays one buffer, while changes to an image are written to the next buffer.

This is the graphics programming version of a cartoon flipbook!

So far, you have one .py file. Eventually your game will be made up of more than one file. The images that you use will each be a separate file in the game folder that you create.

We have created assets for this game. You should use these assets while completing the tutorial. Once you get to the *Break Your Game* section (page 249), you are encouraged to try out your own assets.

Downloading and Storing Assets

1. Go to **OddDot.com/codethisgame**.

2. Find the assets and click **download asset package**.

3. Find the zipped file in your **downloads**.

4. Extract the files by:

   Mac - right click on the folder then select **open**.

   Windows - right click on the folder then select **extract all**.

5. Drag each asset out of the folder and drop it into **vampire_pizza_directory**.

> **Power Up:** Each asset file must be in the same directory as your game file.

Load Assets into Your Program

Now that you have your assets saved in your game folder, you can use them in your game. You will use `image.load()` to add the image into your program.

Loading assets is part of our game setup phase.

Game Setup

1. Import any libraries that we need
2. Initialize Pygame
3. Create a game window
4. Create global constants
5. **Load assets**
6. Create game objects
7. Initialize game objects

```
#Create the game window
GAME_WINDOW = display.set_mode(WINDOW_RES)
display.set_caption('Attack of the Vampire Pizzas!')

#Set up the enemy image
#Load the image into the program
pizza_img = image.load('vampire.png')
#Convert the image to a surface
pizza_surf = Surface.convert_alpha(pizza_img)

#------------------------------------------------
#Game loop

game_running = True
while game_running:
```

Take a Closer Look

Do you see the pattern?

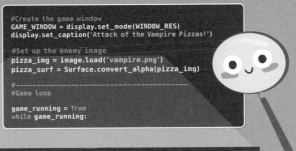

```
#Create the game window
GAME_WINDOW = display.set_mode(WINDOW_RES)
display.set_caption('Attack of the Vampire Pizzas!')

#Set up the enemy image
pizza_img = image.load('vampire.png')
pizza_surf = Surface.convert_alpha(pizza_img)

#------------------------------------------------
#Game loop

game_running = True
while game_running:
```

```
pizza_img = image.load('vampire.png')
```

variable name

object

method

argument

We store the image in a variable so that we don't have to type the whole method every time we want to access the image.

The `Surface.convert_alpha()` method changes the image pixels into the same format that our game window uses. This will prevent problems later.

What Is a Surface in Pygame?

In Pygame, you will use **surfaces** often.
A surface is a flat object. A surface is like a blank piece of paper. On the paper, you can have an image, a color, or a drawing. When you load the image of the pizza, you are creating a surface in Pygame. In your game, you will have many surfaces on the screen at once. This pizza will be one of your game components. Surfaces can't interact with one another. The surface is just one part of the vampire pizza sprite that we will create.

Resize and Display Image

>>> Type This

```
#Set up the enemy image
pizza_img = image.load('vampire.png')
pizza_surf = Surface.convert_alpha(pizza_img)
VAMPIRE_PIZZA = transform.scale(pizza_surf, (100, 100))
GAME_WINDOW.blit(VAMPIRE_PIZZA, (150, 150))

#-------------------------------------------------
#Game loop

game_running = True
while game_running:
```

Take a Closer Look

```
#Set up the enemy image
pizza_img = image.load('vampire.png')
pizza_surf = Surface.convert_alpha(pizza_img)
VAMPIRE_PIZZA = transform.scale(pizza_surf, (100, 100))
GAME_WINDOW.blit(VAMPIRE_PIZZA, (150, 150))

#------------------------------------------
#Game loop

game_running = True
while game_running:
```

`VAMPIRE_PIZZA = transform.scale(pizza_surf, (100, 100))`

This method adjusts the size of our image to be **100** pixels wide and **100** pixels high.

Notice the second argument is a tuple that contains both the width and height of the surface.

The `blit()` method tells the program to display an image to the screen. In programming, to  an image means to display it to the screen.

Take a look at the signature:

GAME_WINDOW.blit(surface, (location tuple))

Test It Out

Check your work and run your file. Can you see the pizza in the upper-left corner of your game window?

Constants

We often use variables to store values that will change over the course of the game. For example, a variable called **score** might start with a value of 0, but the value would change as the player scores points. Other times we use variables because we are going to use that value many times during the game. The value won't change during the game, but if we want to make an adjustment to the value, we only need to change it in one place instead of everywhere that it is used. For example, we could use the variable **WIDTH = 100** to set the width of several sprites in the game. Assuming that the sprites do not change size during gameplay, this is called a **constant**, because the value stays the same during gameplay.

As you build your game, pay attention to the capitalization of variable names. Most of the time, we create variable names that are all lowercase. To keep track of the important constants in our game, we will use all uppercase variable names and put them toward the top of the program. Capitalization doesn't change how the program runs, but it does help us keep our programs organized and readable.

Review: How to Run My File

Remember to run your program:

Save your file by pressing **ctrl/cmd + s.**

In the command line type `python name_file.py`. So in this case, type `python VampirePizzaAttack.py`.

Hit **enter/return.**

You should either see your game window or get an error message in the shell.

Grace's Corner

Spaces v. Tabs

Have you ever gotten an error message with the word *unindent*?

This word is a clue to you that there is an error with your indentation somewhere. Make sure the line of code is indented with the correct amount of spaces. Does it line up with the other code in the loop or conditional?

If you think the indentation is correct but you are still getting the same error, you might be mixing your tabs and spaces!

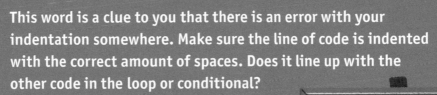

DON'T MIX TABS & SPACES!

In this book, we will use spaces to indent. You could go back and retype all of the indented code with four spaces in front, or you could use one of your IDE's built-in tools. In IDLE, you can select **Edit → Replace**. In the **Find** box, type in a tab. In the **Replace** box, type in four spaces. You won't see anything in the boxes, but if you click the **Replace+Find** button, it will find all the tabs and replace them with spaces for you!

Using the Coordinate System

You may be used to the coordinate plane that you learned in school. Remember how to plot **x** and **y** coordinates using this system? The red dot in the image is at coordinate **(6, 4)**. This means if you move your finger along the x-axis to **6**, then up **4**, you should land on the dot.

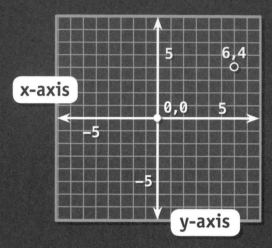

In graphics programming, we still use **x** and **y** coordinates, but the plane is laid out a bit differently. On this coordinate plane, **(0,0)** is in the upper-left corner. You won't need to worry about negative numbers.

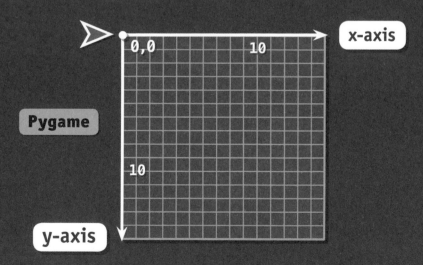

If you move your finger to the right along the x-axis, the numbers will go up until you reach the width of your game window. If your game window has a width of **500**, then the x-coordinates will be between **0** and **500**.

If you move your finger down along the y-axis, the numbers will go up until you reach the height of your game window. If your game window has a height of **300**, then the y-coordinates will be between **0** and **300**.

Just like in your math class, the coordinates are always listed in the same order **(x,y)**.

Try finding **(7,10)** on the Pygame coordinate plane.

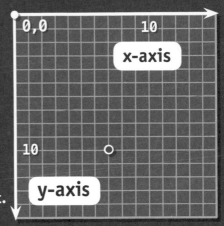

If you are unsure what coordinates to use, you can always start by guessing and then make adjustments by trial and error until you find the coordinates that you want.

Refactor

Change Game Window and Blit Location

1. Try changing the game window to a larger size: **1100** wide and **600** high.

2. Blit the pizza sprite to the location `(900, 400)` in the lower-right corner of the game window.

Try to refactor on your own before you check your work.

```
#Create the game window
GAME_WINDOW = display.set_mode(WINDOW_RES)
display.set_caption('Attack of the Vampire Pizzas!')

#Set up the enemy image
pizza_img = image.load('vampire.png')
pizza_surf = Surface.convert_alpha(pizza_img)
VAMPIRE_PIZZA = transform.scale(pizza_surf, (100, 100))

#Display the enemy image to the screen
GAME_WINDOW.blit(VAMPIRE_PIZZA, (900,400))
#------------------------------------------------
#Game loop

#Define the conditions for running the loop
game_running = True

#Start game loop
while game_running:
```

Attack of the Vampire Pizzas!

Level Up!

0 1 2 3 4 5 6 7 8 9 10 11 12 13 ★

Great job! You are now able to add images to your game!

Chapter 3
Drawing Shapes

In this chapter, you will get your pizza ready for delivery as you learn how to draw shapes. By the time you complete level 3, you will be able to:

1. Draw a circle

2. Draw a rectangle

3. Add a background image to your game

Another way to add graphics to your game is by drawing. In this chapter, you will learn how to create basic shapes and you will add your background image.

Pygame comes with built-in methods that create basic shapes. Let's play with a few of them. Later on, you will use squares to create a background grid for your game.

Practice Drawing Shapes

Each shape has its own method attached to the **Draw** object. Draw is a toolkit for—you guessed it—drawing! Each method has several arguments that must be passed to the method in order.

First let's create a practice file. With your **VampirePizzaAttack.py** file open, go to the upper-right corner of your code editor and select **File → Save As.** Name the new file **prepare_pizza.py**.

Okay, now we're ready to practice making shapes. We're going to use shapes to prepare our pizza for delivery.

Let's add a giant pepperoni by creating a circle.

>>> **Type This**

```
VAMPIRE_PIZZA = transform.scale(pizza_surf, (100, 100))

#Display the enemy image to the screen
GAME_WINDOW.blit(VAMPIRE_PIZZA, (1100, 600))

#Add a giant pepperoni
draw.circle(GAME_WINDOW, (255, 0, 0), (925, 425), 25, 0)

#Draw a green rectangle
draw.rect(GAME_WINDOW, (0, 255, 0), (25, 25, 50, 25), 5)

#To Do: Change the arguments in the rectangle above to
#create a pizza box

#To Do: Add the lid of the pizza box here

#---------------------------------------------------------
#Game loop

game_running = True
while game_running:
```

Take a Closer Look

Take a look at the signature for a circle below. The arguments need to be in the same order every time you code a circle.

draw.circle(surface, color, location, radius, border)

This is the object. It's the Draw tool kit.

This is the first argument. It tells the program which surface to draw the circle on.

This is the third argument. The (x, y) coordinate will be the center point of the circle.

```
draw.circle(GAME_WINDOW, (255, 0, 0), (925, 425), 25, 0)
```

This is the method. We have chosen a circle.

This is the second argument. These numbers represent a color using the **RGB** values. (See the box on page 86.)

This is the fourth argument. It sets the size of the radius of the circle.

This is the fifth argument. It sets the thickness of the border. If we set it to 0, it will fill in the circle.

Test It Out

Run your program to see what you've created. Type `python prepare_pizza.py` in the terminal window. It should be a giant pepperoni on our vampire pizza! If not, stop and debug.

RGB stands for **Red Green Blue**. It is a number system that digital designers use to create colors on the computer. Each letter can range from zero to 255. No color is 0, and **255** is the brightest possible color.

(255, 0, 0)	(0, 255, 0)	(0, 0, 255)
RED	**GREEN**	**BLUE**

All the colors that you need can be created with these numbers. You can always find codes for any RGB color online. If you search for "RGB codes," you will find color pickers and charts that will help you find codes for the exact color you would like to use.

Take a Closer Look

```
VAMPIRE_PIZZA = transform.scale (pizza_surf, (100, 100))

#Display the vampire pizza
GAME_WINDOW.blit(VAMPIRE_PIZZA, (1100, 600))

#Adds a giant pepperoni
draw.circle(GAME_WINDOW, (255, 0, 0), (925, 425), 25, 0)

#Draws a green rectangle
draw.rect(game_window, (0, 255, 0), (25, 25, 50, 25), 5)

#Game loop
game_running = True
while game_running:
```

Let's take a look at the signature for a rectangle.

draw.rect(surface, color, location/size tuple, border)

Now look at the rectangle in our program:

```
draw.rect(game_window, (0, 255, 0), (25, 25, 50, 25), 5)
```

TUPLE   TUPLE

Notice the size/location **tuple**. In a tuple, the items are always in the same order. The first two numbers are the (x, y) coordinate of the upper-left corner of the rectangle. The second two numbers are the width and height of the rectangle. So it sets both our location and size. The RGB code that sets the color is also a tuple.

25, 25

25

50

▶ Your Turn

Can you change the arguments in the rectangle you just added to create a pizza box around your vampire pizza?

Adding a Pizza Box

Change the color tuple and the location/size tuple to make it look like the pizza is in a cardboard pizza box.

1. To make brown, try the RGB code `(160, 82, 45)`. You can adjust each number to change the shade.

2. Test the location and size until it makes a border around the pizza.

Test It Out

Run your file to check your work. Remember that you will probably have to debug more than once to get it right.

Adding a Lid

3. Use another `draw.rect()` method to create an open lid above the pizza box, as shown in the screenshot. Run your file to check your work and debug.

```python
VAMPIRE_PIZZA = transform.scale(pizza_surf, (100, 100))

#Display the enemy image to the screen
GAME_WINDOW.blit(VAMPIRE_PIZZA, (900,400))

#Add a giant pepperoni
draw.circle(GAME_WINDOW, (255, 0, 0), (925, 425), 25, 0)
#Put it in a pizza box
draw.rect(GAME_WINDOW, (160, 82, 45), (895, 395, 110, 110), 5)
#Give it a lid
draw.rect(GAME_WINDOW, (160, 82, 45), (895, 295, 110, 110), 0)


#--------------------------------------------------------
#Game loop

#Define the conditions for running the game loop
game_running = True

#Start game loop
while game_running:
```

Now that you've learned how to draw shapes, let's continue with the game. Go back to your **VampirePizzaAttack.py** game file.

Add Your Background Image

Now you will add a background image to your game. In a previous chapter we downloaded the assets package and stored it in the same directory as your game file. Check to see that the file **restaurant.jpg** is in **vampire_pizza_directory**.

Find the place in your code where you added the image of the vampire pizza enemy. You will use these three lines of code as a model for adding the background image.

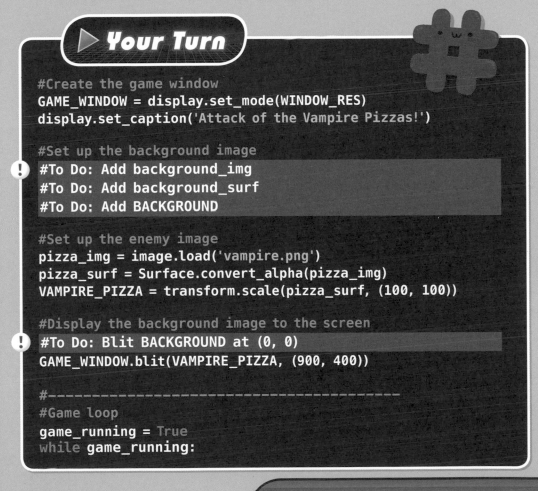

▷ **Your Turn**

```
#Create the game window
GAME_WINDOW = display.set_mode(WINDOW_RES)
display.set_caption('Attack of the Vampire Pizzas!')

#Set up the background image
#To Do: Add background_img
#To Do: Add background_surf
#To Do: Add BACKGROUND

#Set up the enemy image
pizza_img = image.load('vampire.png')
pizza_surf = Surface.convert_alpha(pizza_img)
VAMPIRE_PIZZA = transform.scale(pizza_surf, (100, 100))

#Display the background image to the screen
#To Do: Blit BACKGROUND at (0, 0)
GAME_WINDOW.blit(VAMPIRE_PIZZA, (900, 400))

#-------------------------------------------------
#Game loop
game_running = True
while game_running:
```

Follow each step below:

1. First load the image `restaurant.jpg` using `image.load()` and store it in a variable called `background_img`. Follow the same pattern that was used to load the pizza image:

   ```
   background_img = image.load('file name of your
   selected background image')
   ```

2. Use `Surface.convert_alpha()` to convert the `background_img` to the correct format. Store it in a variable called `background_surf`.

3. Use `transform.scale()` to set the size of the image. Store it in a variable called `BACKGROUND`.

4. Now you can `blit()` the image to the `GAME_WINDOW`:

   ```
   GAME_WINDOW.blit(BACKGROUND, (0,0))
   ```

Power Up: Use `WINDOW_RES` to set the (width, height) of `BACKGROUND`. This will make it the same size as our game window.

Check Your Work

TEST
BUILD
PLAN

```
#Create the game window
GAME_WINDOW = display.set_mode(WINDOW_RES)
display.set_caption('Attack of the Vampire Pizzas!')

#Set up the background image
background_img = image.load('restaurant.jpg')
background_surf = Surface.convert_alpha(background_img)
BACKGROUND = transform.scale(background_surf, WINDOW_RES)
```

```
#Set up the enemy image
pizza_img = image.load('vampire.png')
pizza_surf = Surface.convert_alpha(pizza_img)
VAMPIRE_PIZZA = transform.scale(pizza_surf, (100, 100))

#Display the background image to the screen
GAME_WINDOW.blit(BACKGROUND, (0,0))
#Display the enemy image to the screen
GAME_WINDOW.blit(VAMPIRE_PIZZA, (900, 400))

#------------------------------------------------
#Game loop

#Define the conditions for running the game loop
game_running = True

#Start game loop
while game_running:
```

Level Up!

0 1 2 ✳3 4 5 6 7 8 9 10 11 12 13 ★

Your game has a background image now! You also know
how to add shapes to your game.

Chapter 4
Background Grid

In our game, we want to be able to know what parts of the background our vampire pizzas are passing over. That way, we can make some parts safe and other parts traps. To do this, there will be two parts of our grid: a part we can see and a part we cannot see.

We are going to create grid lines that overlay the background image. This is the part that we can see. Then we'll create a layer of the grid that makes it interactive. This part of the grid is important because it is the part that the other game components, like pizzas, can interact with. We can mark parts of it as safe or as trap zones.

> ### In this chapter, you will:
>
> 1. Create grid lines over the background image.
>
> 2. Create an interactive background grid.

Visible Grid

Let's start with the layer of the grid that we can see. We'll add the interactive part of the grid in a later chapter.

Before we draw the grid, we are going to create variables for the color of our grid lines and the size of our grid tiles.

```
WINDOW_WIDTH = 1100
WINDOW_HEIGHT = 600
WINDOW_RES = (WINDOW_WIDTH, WINDOW_HEIGHT)

#Define tile parameters
WIDTH = 100
#To Do: Add HEIGHT here

#Define colors
WHITE = (255, 255, 255)

#-------------------------------------------------
#Load assets

#Create the game window
GAME_WINDOW = display.set_mode(WINDOW_RES)
display.set_caption('Attack of the Vampire Pizzas!')
```

▶ Your Turn

1. Create the `HEIGHT` variable on your own.

2. The titles are squares, so they should have equal sides.

You can check your work at the end of the chapter.

Refactor

Remember, anytime that we have a value that we might want to change later, we need a variable.

For example, you may want to adjust the size of the pizza later on.

The vampire pizza and other sprites in our game will be the same size as a tile, so we can use the same `HEIGHT` and `WIDTH` variables.

Delete the argument `(100, 100)` and replace it with the variables we just created.

```
#Set up the enemy image
pizza_img = image.load('vampire.png')
pizza_surf = Surface.convert_alpha(pizza_img)
VAMPIRE_PIZZA = transform.scale(pizza_surf, (100, 100))
VAMPIRE_PIZZA = transform.scale(pizza_surf, (WIDTH, HEIGHT))

GAME_WINDOW.blit(BACKGROUND, (0, 0))
GAME_WINDOW.blit(VAMPIRE_PIZZA, (900, 400))

#-----------------------------------------------
#Game loop
game_running = True
while game_running:
```

It is important to define any variables above the code that uses them.
The program executes from the top to bottom. For example, the
program won't know what **WIDTH** or **HEIGHT** mean if it executes
the **transform.scale()** method before the variable is defined.

Drawing the Grid

We're going to use two loops to draw the grid. Let's start by just
drawing a single tile in the upper-left corner.
Follow the steps to add the new code.

```
pizza_img = image.load('vampire.png')
pizza_surf = Surface.convert_alpha(pizza_img)
VAMPIRE_PIZZA = transform.scale(pizza_surf, (WIDTH, HEIGHT))

#-----------------------------------------------
#Initialize and draw background grid
#To Do: Create tile_color variable here
#To Do: Draw rectangle here

GAME_WINDOW.blit(BACKGROUND, (0, 0))
GAME_WINDOW.blit(VAMPIRE_PIZZA, (900, 400))
#-----------------------------------------------
#Game loop
game_running = True
while game_running:
```

1. Create a variable called `tile_color` and set the value to **WHITE**.

2. Use the pattern for a rectangle to draw the first tile in your program:

   draw.rect(surface, color, location/size, border)

3. Draw this rectangle to **BACKGROUND**.

4. Use the variable `tile_color` for the color argument.

5. Set the location to **0, 0** and use **WIDTH** and **HEIGHT** for size.

6. The border size should be **1**.

Check Your Work

```
tile_color = WHITE
draw.rect(BACKGROUND, tile_color, (0, 0, WIDTH, HEIGHT), 1)
```

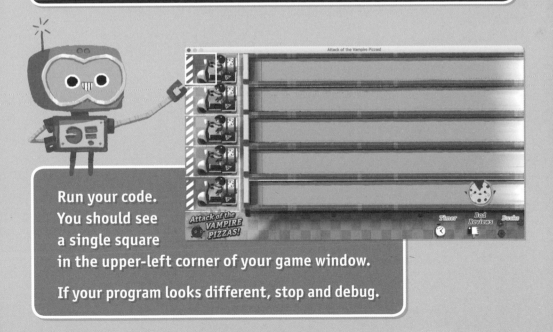

Run your code. You should see a single square in the upper-left corner of your game window.

If your program looks different, stop and debug.

Loops

Loops allow us to run a snippet of code repeatedly. There are two types of loops that we will use in Python: **while loops** and **for loops**. Let's take a closer look at **for loops**.

A **for loop** is a block of code that runs a specified number of times. The number is indicated by a range: `for number in range(6):` or a list: `for item in list:`

Let's look at an example from a program that makes pizza. These snippets won't run on their own or in your program. Let's take a look at what code for making a pizza might look like without a loop.

Make Pizza

We start with three pizzas:

```
pizza_0 = PizzaObject()
pizza_1 = PizzaObject()
pizza_2 = PizzaObject()
```

For each pizza, we'll run methods that **apply_sauce**, **apply_cheese**, **apply_toppings**, **cook** the pizza, and **slice** the pizza into eight pieces.

```
pizza_0.apply_sauce()
pizza_0.apply_cheese()
pizza_0.apply_toppings()
pizza_0.cook()
pizza_0.slice()
pizza_0.slice()
pizza_0.slice()
pizza_0.slice()
```

Now we'll do the same process for the second pizza.

```
pizza_1.apply_sauce()
pizza_1.apply_cheese()
pizza_1.apply_toppings()
pizza_1.cook()
pizza_1.slice()
pizza_1.slice()
pizza_1.slice()
pizza_1.slice()
```

And we'll do the whole thing again for the last pizza:

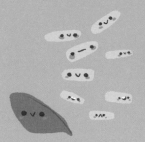

```
pizza_2.apply_sauce()
pizza_2.apply_cheese()
pizza_2.apply_toppings()
pizza_2.cook()
pizza_2.slice()
pizza_2.slice()
pizza_2.slice()
pizza_2.slice()
```

Make Pizza with a Loop

That is a lot of code to write! Instead of typing out the list of steps three times, we can put the same steps into a loop. Let's see what happens.

We start with a list of all three of our pizzas:

```
pizzas = [pizza_0, pizza_1, pizza_2]
```

For each pizza in the list, we follow the steps inside the loop. The loop will run three times, once for each item in the list above. Each time the loop runs, we call it an **iteration**.

```
pizzas = [pizza_0, pizza_1, pizza_2]
for pizza in pizzas:
    pizza.apply_sauce()
    pizza.apply_cheese()
    pizza.apply_toppings()
    pizza.cook()
    pizza.slice()
    pizza.slice()
    pizza.slice()
    pizza.slice()
```

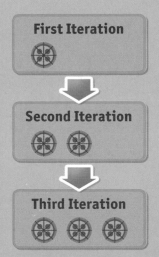

First Iteration

Second Iteration

Third Iteration

 Loops make code more efficient and easier to write.

Use a Loop to Draw Tiles

Now that you have a single tile, we are going to use a **loop** to create six tiles, one for each row of our grid. By using a loop, we don't need to draw each square in a separate line of code.

To create the first tile for each row, we're going to use a **for loop** that draws a rectangle six times. A row goes across. The column goes up and down.

We are going to make the following changes to your code:

1. Add the loop above your rectangle.

2. Indent the rectangle four spaces.

3. Change the y-coordinate from `0` to `HEIGHT * row`.

>>> **Type This**

```
pizza_surf = Surface.convert_alpha(pizza_img)
VAMPIRE_PIZZA = transform.scale(pizza_surf, (WIDTH, HEIGHT))

#---------------------------------------------
#Initialize and draw background grid

tile_color = WHITE
draw.rect(BACKGROUND, tile_color, (0, 0, WIDTH, HEIGHT), 1)

for row in range(6):
#Notice this method is broken up into two lines
    draw.rect(BACKGROUND, tile_color, (0, HEIGHT * row,
              WIDTH, HEIGHT), 1)

GAME_WINDOW.blit(BACKGROUND, (0, 0))
GAME_WINDOW.blit(VAMPIRE_PIZZA, (900,400))

#---------------------------------------------
#Game loop
game_running = True
while game_running:
```

Take a Closer Look

Let's take a closer look at the change to the location/size tuple. The tuple is a list of the x-coordinate of the upper-left corner, the y-coordinate of the upper-left corner, the width, and the height. Why can't we leave the location coordinates at 0, 0? If we do this, our program will draw a square six times in the exact same place! It will look like one square to us.

The word *row* is a list of items in a range of 6. You can imagine the list like this:

row_list = [row_0, row_1, row_2, row_3, row_4, row_5]

Remember, computers start counting at 0. So there are six items in the list, but they are labeled 0 to 5. Our x-coordinate for each square will be 0. Our y-coordinate is 100 (the height) multiplied by the row number from our list. Take a look at the (x,y) coordinates for each rectangle:

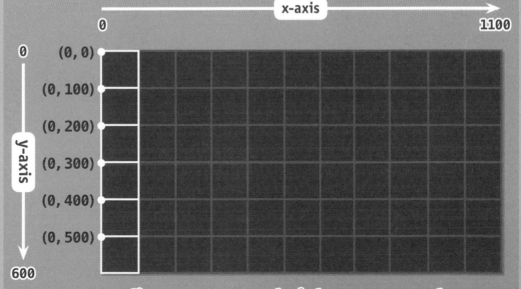

y-coordinate = square height x row number

Stop and run your code to see if you get the first square for all six rows. If you don't need to stop and debug, move on to making columns!

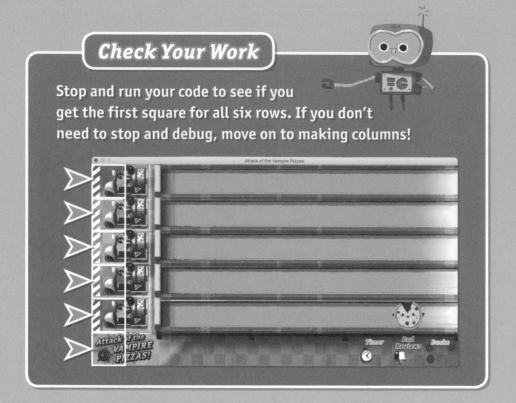

Nested Loops

A **nested loop** is a loop inside a loop.

Let's think back to our pizza-making example. We simplified our pizza-making by using a loop. This is what the example code in our imaginary pizza-making program looked like:

```python
pizzas = [pizza_0, pizza_1, pizza_2]
for pizza in pizzas:
    pizza.apply_sauce()
    pizza.apply_cheese()
    pizza.apply_toppings()
    pizza.cook()
    pizza.slice()
    pizza.slice()
    pizza.slice()
    pizza.slice()
```

Make Pizza with Nested Loops

We can simplify our pizza-making code even further by adding another loop inside the first loop.

```python
pizzas = [pizza_0, pizza_1, pizza_2]
for pizza in pizzas:
    pizza.apply_sauce()
    pizza.apply_cheese()
    pizza.apply_toppings()
    pizza.cook()
    #Slice the pizza four times
    for i in range(4):
        pizza.slice()
```

Instead of running the `pizza.slice()` command four times, we can put it in a loop with a range of four. In the loop, the letter `i` is a placeholder variable. This just says, "Run the code in this loop once for each number in the range." In this case, the code will run four times. Each time the main loop, `for pizza in pizzas:`, iterates, this nested loop, `for i in range(4):`, will iterate four times.

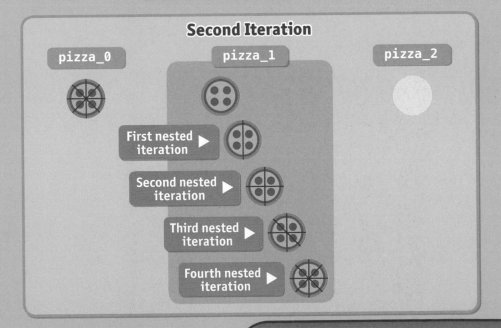

Second Iteration

pizza_0   pizza_1   pizza_2

First nested iteration ▶

Second nested iteration ▶

Third nested iteration ▶

Fourth nested iteration ▶

Add Columns

Now that we've created the first tile of all six rows, we need to draw tiles across each row so that we end up with eleven columns across the screen. To do that, we need to use a **nested loop**.

We are going to make the following changes to your code:

1. Add a **for loop** inside the first loop. This loop will loop through a list of eleven columns. We'll indent this loop four spaces.

2. Make sure that your rectangle is inside both loops. That means it needs to be indented 8 spaces (4 for each loop).

3. Change the x-coordinate in the location/direction tuple so that the x-coordinate of each rectangle changes for each column.

>>> **Type This**

```
pizza_surf = Surface.convert_alpha(pizza_img)
VAMPIRE_PIZZA = transform.scale(pizza_surf, (WIDTH, HEIGHT))

#-------------------------------------------------
#Initialize and draw background grid

tile_color = WHITE
for row in range(6):
    draw.rect(BACKGROUND, tile_color, (0, HEIGHT*row,
            WIDTH, HEIGHT), 1)

    for column in range(11):
        draw.rect(BACKGROUND, tile_color, (WIDTH*column,
            HEIGHT*row, WIDTH, HEIGHT), 1)

GAME_WINDOW.blit(BACKGROUND, (0, 0))
GAME_WINDOW.blit(VAMPIRE_PIZZA, (900, 400))

#-------------------------------------------------
#Game loop
game_running = True
while game_running:
```

Grace's Corner

There are two complex parts of our code that can trip up even seasoned professionals. If you're having trouble running your program, take a closer look at these two areas:

1. Indentation in nested loops

0 spaces in front of line

```
tile_color = WHITE
for row in range(6):
    for column in range(11):
        draw.rect(BACKGROUND, tile_color,
                (WIDTH * column, HEIGHT * row, WIDTH, HEIGHT), 1)
```

4 spaces in front of line

8 spaces in front of line

2. Syntax of arguments with multiple data types

Make sure all parentheses come in pairs.

These parentheses surround all of the arguments.

Location/size tuple

Each item in the tuple is separated by a comma.

```
draw.rect(surface, color, (x, y, WIDTH, HEIGHT), border)
```

These parentheses surround the location/size tuple.

Each argument is separated by a comma.

```
draw.rect(BACKGROUND, tile_color,
        (WIDTH * column, HEIGHT * row, WIDTH, HEIGHT), 1)
```

Check Your Work

Run your code to check your work and debug.

```python
#Define game window parameters
WINDOW_WIDTH = 1100
WINDOW_HEIGHT = 600
WINDOW_RES = (WINDOW_WIDTH, WINDOW_HEIGHT)

#Define the tile parameters
WIDTH = 100
HEIGHT = 100

#Define colors
WHITE = (255, 255, 255)


#----------------------------------------------
#Load assets

#Create the game window
GAME_WINDOW = display.set_mode(WINDOW_RES)
display.set_caption('Attack of the Vampire Pizzas!')

#Set up the background image
background_img = image.load('restaurant.jpg')
background_surf = Surface.convert_alpha(background_img)
BACKGROUND = transform.scale(background_surf, WINDOW_RES)

#Set up the enemy image
pizza_img = image.load('vampire.png')
pizza_surf = Surface.convert_alpha(pizza_img)
VAMPIRE_PIZZA = transform.scale(pizza_surf, (WIDTH, HEIGHT))

#----------------------------------------------
#Initialize and draw the background grid

#Define the color of the grid outline
tile_color = WHITE
```

```python
#Populate the background grid
for row in range(6):
    for column in range(11):
        draw.rect(BACKGROUND, tile_color, (WIDTH * column,
                  HEIGHT * row, WIDTH, HEIGHT), 1)

#Display the background image to the screen
GAME_WINDOW.blit(BACKGROUND, (0,0))
#Display the enemy image to the screen
GAME_WINDOW.blit(VAMPIRE_PIZZA, (900, 400))


#------------------------------------------------
#Game loop

#Define the conditions for running the loop
game_running = True

#Start game loop
while game_running:
```

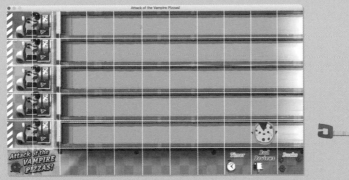

Level Up!

0 1 2 3 **4** 5 6 7 8 9 10 11 12 13 ★

You've used *loops* to add an interactive grid to your game!

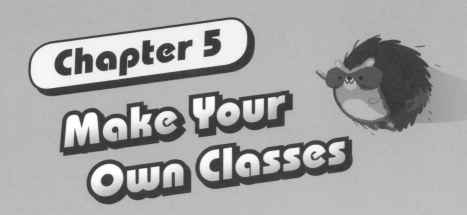

Chapter 5
Make Your Own Classes

Let's pause before moving on with the game. We've learned quite a bit about objects and methods. So far, you have used objects and methods that are built into Python, but you can also make your own. We're going to learn to do that right now.

Create a new practice file by selecting **File → New File** from your text editor. Name the new file **MonsterFoods.py**. During this chapter, be sure to work only in the **MonsterFoods.py** file.

Ideas for Programmers

Classes create new **objects** that we can use in our code. **Classes** are made up of data about an object (**attributes**) and rules that guide an object's behavior (**methods**). For example, a new object type could be **Pets**. Pets would be the name of our **class**. We can use **attributes** to store information about the object. **Attributes** are traits that the new object has. For example, information about dogs could include their breed and name. We will also want to give the object a set of rules. The name for the set of rules is **methods**. **Methods** are usually actions that the new object can do. For example, a dog might be able to do tricks like speak or roll over.

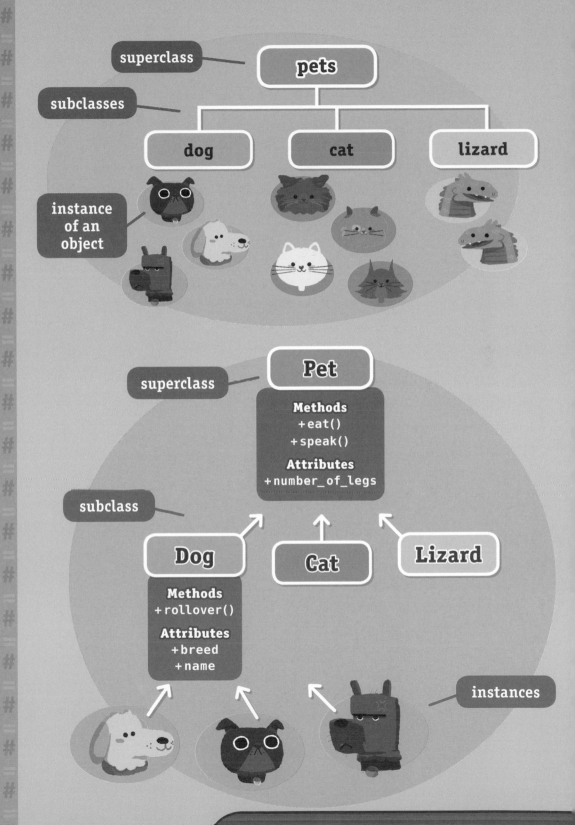

superclass

pets

subclasses

dog

cat

lizard

instance of an object

superclass

Pet

Methods
+eat()
+speak()

Attributes
+number_of_legs

subclass

Dog

Methods
+rollover()

Attributes
+breed
+name

Cat

Lizard

instances

Let's create our own class now. Why don't we create a class of other monster foods? We already have vampire pizzas. What about FrankenBurgers? Or CrummyMummies and WereWatermelons?

Each of these monster types is a separate **subclass** of the base class Monster. Our class Monster will define information about all monsters made of food and how they all behave.

We will create subclasses of different types of monster foods, like FrankenBurgers, with their own specific behaviors. All monster foods can say what type of monster they are, and they each love to eat something different that spooks humans. For example, the **VampirePizza** subclass drinks all the pizza sauce, and the **FrankenBurger** subclass eats the hamburger and leaves only the bun.

Let's look at the pattern for creating a new class:

```
class ClassName(object):
```

The line has to end in a colon. Everything indented under this line of code is part of our rules for the new object.

The keyword **class** tells Python we're about to define a new class.

This is the name of the new class. The name is up to the programmer.

This argument tells Python the base class. Unless you are creating a subclass, your base class will be **object**. You don't need to write the word **object**, but it is included here as an example.

>>> Type This

```
#Create the superclass
class Monster(object):
#Set up the class attribute, the same for all instances
    eats = 'food'
#Define the __init__method
    def __init__(self, name):
#Set up an instance attribute, different for each instance
        self.name = name
#Define a method for speaking behavior
    def speak(self):
        print(self.name + ' speaks')
#Define a method for eating behavior
    def eat(self, meal):
        if meal == self.eats:
            print('yum!')
        else:
            print('blech!')
#Create an instance of MonsterFood
my_monster = Monster('Spooky Snack')
#Call the methods on the new instance
my_monster.speak()
my_monster.eat('food')
```

BUILD
PLAN
TEST

Take a Closer Look

Inside the new class type:

```
class Monster(object):
    eats = 'food'
    def __init__(self, name):
        self.name = name
    def speak(self):
        print(self.name + ' speaks')
    def eat(self, meal):
        if meal == self.eats:
            print('yum!')
        else:
            print('blech!')
my_monster = Monster('Spooky Snack')
my_monster.speak()
my_monster.eat('food')
```

```
class Monster(object):
    eats = 'food'
```

eats is a **class attribute**. Remember, **attributes** store data about the object. They are variables that are specific to a class. The attribute called **eats** stores the food that Monster objects like. Since Monster isn't a specific kind of monster, we can just say that Monster objects eat **'food'**. Everything that belongs to this class needs to be indented 4 spaces so that Python knows it is part of the class Monster.

```
class Monster(object):
    eats = 'food'
    def __init__(self, name):
```

def is a keyword that is short for **define**. It tells Python that we are defining a new method. The method is indented 4 spaces.

The first method of a new class is a special method called **__init__**. **init** is short for **initialize** and is surrounded by two underscores on either side. This method sets the rules for creating instances of the Monster class and will be called every time you initialize an instance in your program.

We'll give each instance of Monster its own name with the argument **(self, name)**. **self** is an argument that every **__init__** method needs. The line has to end in a colon **:**.

```python
def __init__(self, name):
    self.name = name
```

This line creates an instance attribute called `name`. The name of each monster instance will be different. Everything that is part of this `__init__` method needs to be indented 4 spaces from where the method starts. So that's 8 spaces total.

The speak and eat methods set up rules for how Monster objects behave. Methods are functions that are specific to a class. These methods follow the same pattern that was used for the `__init__` method.

```python
def speak(self):
    print(self.name + ' speaks')
def eat(self, meal):
    if meal == self.eats:
        print('yum!')
    else:
        print('blech!')
```

The method `speak` prints the name of the Monster instance with a message. We will define what each type of monster should say when we set up the Monster subclasses.

The next method will give rules for what the monster does when it eats.

The method `eat` tests if the meal given to the monster matches the **eats** attribute. That attribute is `'food'`. If we give the monster `'food'`, it will print `'yum!'`. If we give the monster anything else to eat, it will print `'blech!'` We will define what kind of meal each type of monster eats when we set up the Monster subclasses.

Before a class can run, we need to do two things: create an instance of the new class, and **call** one or more of the methods. First you give the program all the rules for what to do. Then you have to tell it when to run those rules.

> To **call** a method means to tell it to run.

Create an Instance of Monster:

```
my_monster = Monster('Spooky Snack')
```

`my_monster` is the variable name of our first instance of Monster.

To create an instance of a class, we have to call the name of the class `Monster`.

`'Spooky Snack'` is the argument we need to pass to the `__init__` method in order to create the instance. Notice we didn't need to put in an argument for `self`. `'Spooky Snack'` is what we will name this instance of Monster. This is called **passing in** an argument.

Call the Methods:

```
my_monster.speak()
```

This is how we call the method `speak()` for the instance `my_monster`. You might recognize this pattern: `object.method(arguments)`. These are the basic building blocks that you learned earlier. Only, in this case, there is no argument to pass in. When this runs, it should print `'Spooky Snack speaks'`.

```
my_monster.eat('food')
```

This is how we call the method `eat()` for the instance `my_monster`. In this case we will give the monster a meal of `'food'`. When this method runs, it should print `'yum!'` because we gave it a meal of `'food'`.

Test It Out

We're not using Pygame, so you won't have a game window pop-up. Instead, look in the terminal window, right below where you ran the file. It should look something like this:

```
Python Shell
File  Edit  Shell  Debug  Options  Window  Help
Python 3
>>>    /Users/VampirePizza/MonsterFood.py
Spooky Snack speaks
yum!
>>>
```

When you are done, **comment out** the instance and method calls by putting a **#** symbol at the start of each line of code. We will not need these lines of code for the rest of our program.

>>> **Type This**

```python
    def eat(self, meal):
        if meal == self.eats:
            print('yum!')
        else:
            print('blech!')
```

```python
my_monster = Monster('Spooky Snack')
my_monster.speak()
my_monster.eat('food')
```

```python
#my_monster = Monster('Spooky Snack')
#my_monster.speak()
#my_monster.eat('food')
```

Subclasses

Let's make this program a little more interesting by adding subclasses. We will add a subclass called **FrankenBurger** together. Then you will add two more subclasses of monster foods on your own. Subclasses follow all the same rules of their base class, unless you decide to override some of those rules.

>>> *Type This*

```python
#Monster Class
    def eat(self, meal):
        if meal == self.eats:
            print('yum!')
        else:
            print('blech!')

#my_monster = Monster('Spooky Snack')
#my_monster.speak()
#my_monster.eat('food')

#Create a subclass of Monster
class FrankenBurger(Monster):
#Set up a class attribute
    eats = 'hamburger patties'
#Define any methods that are different from the superclass
    def speak(self):
        print('My name is ' + self.name + 'Burger')
```

Take a Closer Look

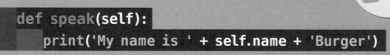

```python
    def speak(self):
        print('My name is ' + self.name + 'Burger')
```

This code overrides the speak method for FrankenBurger. Instead of printing `self.name + 'speaks'`, FrankenBurgers will print `'My name is ' + self.name + 'Burger'`.

Notice that we did not make any changes to the `init` or `eat` methods, so they will run exactly the same way for FrankenBurger that they do for the entire Monster base class.

Special note: When you create a subclass, you must have the base class as argument, as in:

```
class FrankenBurger(Monster):
```

When you create a class based on object, this is not considered a subclass and does not need an argument. You would normally write a class like this:

```
class Monster:
```

In this book, we will write it like this instead:

```
class Monster(object):
```

The code will work the same way, and this will help to remind us what the base class is even if it is the default base class **object**.

Test FrankenBurger

You can test the FrankenBurger subclass by setting up an instance of FrankenBurger and calling the methods **speak** and **eat**.

>>> **Type This**

```
class FrankenBurger(Monster):
    eats = 'hamburger patties'
    def speak(self):
        print('My name is ' + self.name + 'Burger')

#Create an instance of FrankenBurger.
#Pass in the name 'Veggiesaurus'
my_frankenburger = FrankenBurger('Veggiesaurus')
#Call the speak method
my_frankenburger.speak()
#Call the eat method. Pass in 'pickles'
my_frankenburger.eat('pickles')
```

When you run the test, the terminal window should print two lines:

`My name is VeggiesaurusBurger` and `blech!`

If you don't see those lines, debug until you do.

When you are done testing the FrankenBurger subclass, comment out the instance and method calls by putting a # symbol at the start of each line of code. When you comment out the code, it should look like this:

```
#my_frankenburger = FrankenBurger('Veggiesaurus')
#my_frankenburger.speak()
#my_frankenburger.eat('pickles')
```

 **Your Turn**

Use the pattern on pages 114–115 to create and test two more subclasses of Monster. Try it on your own. If you get stuck, go to the Check Your Work section on page 121.

1. The first subclass you add will be called `CrummyMummy`. CrummyMummy eats `'chocolate chips'` and should print `'My name is ' + self.name + 'Mummy'` when it speaks.

2. The next subclass you add will be called `WereWatermelon`. WereWatermelon eats `'watermelon juice'` and says `'My name is Were' + self.name`.

3. Test both the CrummyMummy and WereWatermelon subclasses by creating an instance and calling both methods. Use the pattern that we used when we tested both Monster and FrankenBurger.

4. When you are done testing your subclasses, comment out the code that you used for the testing.

Make It Interactive

We can make the program interactive by asking for input from the user. We will use only one line of code that can set up an instance for any of our three subclasses.

```
class WereWatermelon(Monster):
    eats = 'watermelon juice'
    def speak(self):
        print('My name is Were' + self.name)

#my_werewatermelon = WereWatermelon('Veggiesaurus')
#my_werewatermelon.speak()
#my_werewatermelon.eat('watermelon juice')
```

+ `monster_selection = input ('What kind of monster do you want to create? Select: frankenburger, crummymummy, or werewatermelon.')`

+ `monster_name = input('What do you want to name your monster?')`

! `#To Do: Add monster_meal here`

▶ Your Turn

1. Use the `input` method to ask the user `'What will you feed your monster?'`.

2. Store the user's answer in a variable called `monster_meal`.

You can check your work at the end of the chapter.

Take a Closer Look

`monster_name = input('What do you want to name your monster?')`

Stores the user's answer in a variable called `monster_name`.

Asks the user what they want to name their monster.

Test It Out You can pause and test if your program is working. Run the program. Answer the questions. Then type the variable names and press enter. Does the program print your answers? If not, debug before moving on.

Look at the sample user answers below to see what gets stored in each variable:

```
What kind of monster do you want to create? crummymummy
What do you want to name your monster? count vonpeanutbutter
What will you feed your monster? chocolate chips
```

If the user typed the above answers, these are the values that would be stored in each variable:

```
monster_selection = 'crummymummy'
monster_name = 'count vonpeanutbutter'
monster_meal = 'chocolate chips'
```

Now we need to tell the program which subclass to select based on the input in **monster_selection**. Add the following code:

>>> **Type This**

```
monster_selection = input('What kind of monster do you want
                          to create? Select: frankenburger,
                          crummymummy, or werewatermelon.')
monster_name = input('What do you want to name your monster?')
monster_meal = input('What will you feed your monster?')

if monster_selection == 'frankenburger':
    monster_type = FrankenBurger
elif monster_selection == 'crummymummy':
    monster_type = CrummyMummy

#To Do: Test for the selection 'werewatermelon'
#To Do: Assign the type WereWatermelon

else:
    monster_type = Monster
```

Use the conditional pattern.

1. Use `elif` to test if the user's `monster_selection` is `'werewatermelon'`.

2. If the test is **True**, assign `WereWatermelon` as the `monster_type`.

Take a Closer Look

```
if monster_selection == 'frankenburger':
    monster_type = FrankenBurger
elif monster_selection == 'crummymummy':
    monster_type = CrummyMummy
elif monster_selection == 'werewatermelon':
    monster_type = WereWatermelon
else:
    monster_type = Monster
```

```
else:
    monster_type = Monster
```

If the user types anything other than the above three options, the program will select the Monster class as the `monster_type`.

Power Up: *When the user types in their answers, spelling and capitalization matter. If the user misspells the* **monster_selection** *or capitalizes any of the letters, then the program will not recognize it and will select the Monster class as the* **monster_type**. *There are ways to account for these types of errors, but they aren't covered in this book.*

Make It Interactive

The last step to complete our program is to create an instance and call the two methods.

```
elif monster_selection == 'werewatermelon':
    monster_type = WereWatermelon
else:
    monster_type = Monster

my_monster = monster_type(monster_name)

#To Do: Call the speak method
#To Do: Call the eat method
```

▶ Your Turn

Use the pattern for calling a method to add the next two statements: **object.method(argument)**.

1. Call the `speak` method for the object `my_monster`. This method doesn't have any arguments.

2. Call the `eat` method for `my_monster`. Pass in `monster_meal` as an argument.

You can check your work on page 121.

Take a Closer Look

`my_monster = monster_type(monster_name)`

In our example, this would be the same as typing:

`my_monster = CrummyMummy('count vonpeanutbutter')`

`my_monster.eat(monster_meal)`

In our example, this would be the same as typing:

`my_monster.eat('chocolate chips')`

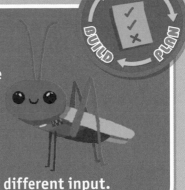

Check Your Work

Run your program and do any debugging that is needed. Once the program runs correctly, run it several times, and try out different test cases.

```python
class Monster(object):
    eats = 'food'
    def __init__(self, name):
        self.name = name
    def speak(self):
        print(self.name + ' speaks')
    def eat(self, meal):
        if meal == self.eats:
            print('yum!')
        else:
            print('blech!')

#my_monster = Monster('Spooky Snack')
#my_monster.speak()
#my_monster.eat('food')

class FrankenBurger(Monster):
    eats = 'hamburger patties'
    def speak(self):
        print('My name is ' + self.name + 'Burger')

#my_frankenburger = FrankenBurger('Veggiesaurus')
#my_frankenburger.speak()
#my_frankenburger.eat('pickles')
```

```python
class CrummyMummy(Monster):
    eats = 'chocolate chips'
    def speak(self):
        print('My name is ' + self.name + 'Mummy')

#my_crummymummy = CrummyMummy('Count VonPeanutbutter')
#my_crummymummy.speak()
#my_crummymummy.eat('chocolate chips')

class WereWatermelon(Monster):
    eats = 'watermelon juice'
    def speak(self):
        print('My name is Were' + self.name)

#my_werewatermelon = WereWatermelon('Rex')
#my_werewatermelon.speak()
#my_werewatermelon.eat('watermelon juice')

monster_selection = input('What kind of monster do you want
                           to create? Select: frankenburger,
                           crummymummy, or werewatermelon')
monster_name = input('What do you want to name your monster?')

monster_meal = input('What will you feed your monster?')


if monster_selection == 'frankenburger':
    monster_type = FrankenBurger
elif monster_selection == 'crummymummy':
    monster_type = CrummyMummy
elif monster_selection == 'werewatermelon':
    monster_type = WereWatermelon
else:
    monster_type = Monster


my_monster = monster_type(monster_name)
my_monster.speak()
my_monster.eat(monster_meal)
```

Note: The output of your program may look slightly different than the example below, because you might have chosen different monster foods and you might have input different answers.

```
Command Prompt                                       □ — ✕

C:\Users\Hedgie\Vampire_Pizza_Directory\MonsterFoods.py
What kind of monster do you want to create? Select:
    frankenburger, crummymummy, or werewatermelon. crummymummy
What do you want to name your monster? CountVonPeanutbutter
What will you feed your monster? chocolate chips
My name is Count VonPeanutbutterMummy
Yum!
```

Level Up!

0 1 2 3 4 **5** 6 7 8 9 10 11 12 13 ★

You can now create your own objects in Python.
You're ready to add sprites to your game! **Excellent!**

Chapter 6

Adding Enemies

The next step in our game development is to add the enemies. We will be trying to prevent vampire pizzas from ending up in our pizza boxes. That would be an unpleasant surprise for our customers!

To add the enemies, you will need to:

1. Create a class of vampire pizzas.

2. Add methods that set up the behavior rules for vampire pizzas.

3. Use the random library to spawn vampire pizzas.

IMPORTANT! We're going back to our game file. Make sure you are working in the file called VampirePizzaAttack.py.

We want to spawn vampire pizzas into random starting rows, otherwise the game would be predictable. To do that, we have to import a new library that will give us the ability to use random numbers in our program.

>>> **Type This**

```
#Import libraries
import pygame
from pygame import *
from random import randint

#Initialize pygame
pygame.init()
```

Now we will be able to spawn vampire pizzas to a random location.

Ideas for Programmers

Random

Because of the way computers work, they can never pick a truly random number. There are many different types of algorithms that simulate random number generation. This is often called **pseudorandom number generation**. Some of these algorithms use sensors to select numbers from the outside world, others use a pattern from a very large number set. For our purposes and for the purposes of most games, using the random library is close enough to random. You won't notice a difference. Modern **cryptography**, the practice of creating and breaking codes, centers on problems related to creating random number sets with computers.

We will create a class of **sprites** called **VampireSprite**. This new class will be based on the Sprite class which is built in to Pygame.

A **sprite** is a game component that can interact with other parts of the game. In Pygame, it's also a class of objects that have special features built in.

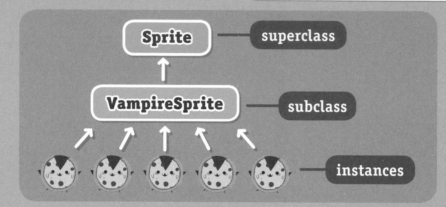

The comment above each line of code explains what that code does. You only need to type the code.

>>> **Type This**

```
pizza_img = image.load('vampire.png')
pizza_surf = Surface.convert_alpha(pizza_img)
VAMPIRE_PIZZA = transform.scale(pizza_surf, (WIDTH, HEIGHT))

#---------------------------------------------
#Set up classes

#Create a subclass of Sprite called VampireSprite
class VampireSprite(sprite.Sprite):

#Define the VampireSprite set-up method
    def __init__(self):
#Take all the behavior rules from the Sprite class and use
#them for VampireSprite
        super().__init__()
#Set the default movement speed
        self.speed = 2
#Randomly select a lane between 0 and 4.
        self.lane = randint(0, 4)
```

BUILD
PLAN
TEST

```
#Add all vampire pizza sprites to a group called all_vampires
    all_vampires.add(self)
#Use the VAMPIRE_PIZZA image as the image for
#vampire pizza sprites
    self.image = VAMPIRE_PIZZA.copy()
#Set each sprite's y-coordinate at the middle of the
#selected lane
    y = 50 + self.lane * 100
#Create a rect for each sprite and place it just off the
#right side of the screen in the correct lane
    self.rect = self.image.get_rect(center = (1100, y))

#To Do: Add update method here
#To Do: Blit the vampire pizza image here

#----------------------------------------------------
#Create class instances and groups

#Create a group for all the VampireSprite instances
all_vampires = sprite.Group()

#----------------------------------------------------
#Initialize and draw the background grid

tile_color = WHITE
for row in range(6):
```

Take a Closer Look

```
pizza_img = image.load ('vampire.png')
pizza_surf = Surface.convert_alpha(pizza_img)
VAMPIRE_PIZZA = transform.scale (pizza_surf, (WIDTH, HEIGHT))

#----------------------------------------------------
#Set up classes
class VampireSprite(sprite.Sprite):

#Define the VampireSprite set-up method
    def __init__(self):
        super().__init__()
        self.speed = 2
        self.lane = randint(0, 4)
        all_vampires.add(self)
```

```
def __init__(self):
```

Inside the class, we define an `__init__` method that only takes
the default argument `self`. Remember, the `__init__` method
creates the rules for setting up new instances of `VampireSprite`.
In this case, each instance is one vampire pizza sprite. In Pygame,
all sprites need a **surface image** and a **rect**. This method sets that
up. It also sets the rules for where new vampire pizza sprites will
spawn. We want vampire pizzas to randomly spawn just off the
right side of the screen to one of five different rows.

Take a Closer Look

```
class VampireSprite(sprite.Sprite):
    #Define the VampireSprite set-up method
    def __init__(self):
        super().__init__()
        self.speed = 2
        self.lane = randint(0, 4)
        all_vampires.add(self)
        self.image = VAMPIRE_PIZZA.copy()
        y = 50 + self.lane * 100
        self.rect = self.image.get_rect(center=(1100, y))
```

super().__init__()

The super() method tells the program that we want to use all the built-in rules for the superclass sprite.Sprite. Anything that we add after this adds new rules specific to the VampireSprite class.

self.rect = self.image.get_rect(center = (1100, y))

In Pygame, adding a rect to an object allows it to interact with other objects in the game. You can think of it as attaching an invisible rectangle to the image.

 **Your Turn**

We will add one more method to the VampireSprite class, and it will be used to display the image of each vampire pizza to the screen.

1. Define a new method called update that takes two arguments: self and game_window.

2. Use blit to display vampire pizza sprites to the game_window. The arguments for the blit method are self.image and (self.rect.x, self.rect.y).

Check Your Work

```
#VampireSprite class, __init__ method
    self.image = VAMPIRE_PIZZA.copy()
    y = 50 + self.lane * 100
    self.rect = self.image.get_rect(center=(1100, y))

    def update(self, game_window):
        game_window.blit(self.image, (self.rect.x, self.rect.y))

#---------------------------------------------
#Create class instances and groups

#Create a group for all the VampireSprite instances
all_vampires = sprite.Group()
```

Take a Closer Look

```
def __init__(self):
    super().__init__()
    self.speed = 2
    self.lane = randint(0, 4)
    all_vampires.add(self)
    self.image = VAMPIRE_PIZZA.copy()
    y = 50 + self.lane * 100
    self.rect = self.image.get_rect(center=(1100, y))
def update(self, game_window):
    game_window.blit(self.image, (self.rect.x, self.rect.y))
```

`self.image`

`(self.rect.x, self.rect.y)`

The object `self` is the placeholder we use when we want to create an attribute that works with every instance of a class. Each sprite will return the same image, `'vampire_pizza.png'`.

All **rects** have a `rect.x` and a `rect.y`. Each sprite will return their current x or y coordinate.

Spawn Vampire Pizza Sprites

You have written all the rules for the VampireSprite class, but you still need to create the instances (individual sprites) and call the update method. We will do this in the game loop.

>>> **Type This**

```
    for event in pygame.event.get():
        if event.type == QUIT:
            game_running = False

#Spawn vampire pizza sprites
    if randint(1, 360) == 1:
        VampireSprite()

#Update displays
    for vampire in all_vampires:
        vampire.update(GAME_WINDOW)

    display.update()

#-------------------------------------------------
#Close main game loop

pygame.quit()
```

Take a Closer Look

```
if randint(1, 360) == 1:
    VampireSprite()
```

The pattern for creating a class instance is: `ClassName()`

Every time the game loop runs, `randint()` will select a number between **1** and **360**. `VampireSprite()` creates one instance every time the computer randomly selects the number **1**. In this case, an instance is one vampire pizza sprite.

```
for vampires in all_vampires:
    vampire.update (GAME_WINDOW)
```

This code updates the location of each vampire pizza sprite once every iteration of the game loop. We added all the sprites to the group called `all_vampires`. This loop goes through each sprite in the group and updates its location on the `GAME_WINDOW`.

Refactor

You might want to change the spawn rate later on to make vampire pizzas appear more or less frequently. To make it easier to change the spawn rate, let's create a variable.

```
#Define tile parameters
WIDTH = 100
HEIGHT = 100

#Define colors
WHITE = (255, 255, 255)

#To Do: Define SPAWN_RATE

#-----------------------------------------------
#Load Assets

#Create window
GAME_WINDOW = display.set_mode(WINDOW_RES)
display.set_caption('Attack of the Vampire Pizzas!')
```

1. Create a new constant variable called `SPAWN_RATE`. Set the value to `360`.

2. Now go back to the game loop and replace the number `360` in `randint()` with `SPAWN_RATE`. You can check your work on the next page.

```
for row in range(6):
    for column in range(11):
        draw.rect(BACKGROUND, tile_color,
                  (WIDTH * column, HEIGHT * row, WIDTH, HEIGHT), 1)

GAME_WINDOW.blit(BACKGROUND, (0,0))
GAME_WINDOW.blit(VAMPIRE_PIZZA, (900,400))

#-----------------------------------------------
#Game loop

game_running = True
while game_running:
```

3. Now that we're spawning vampire pizzas in the game loop, we can remove the line of code we were using before to blit just one pizza to the screen.

Check Your Work

Stop and run your code. You should see vampire pizzas appearing on the right-hand side of the screen. They won't move just yet.

```
#Define tile parameters
WIDTH = 100
HEIGHT = 100

#Define colors
WHITE = (255, 255, 255)

#Set up rates
SPAWN_RATE = 360

#------------------------------------------------
#Load assets

#Create the game window
GAME_WINDOW = display.set_mode(WINDOW_RES)
display.set_caption('Attack of the Vampire Pizzas!')
```

```
#Set up the enemy image
pizza_img = image.load('vampire.png')
pizza_surf = Surface.convert_alpha(pizza_img)
VAMPIRE_PIZZA = transform.scale(pizza_surf, (WIDTH, HEIGHT))

#------------------------------------------------
#Set up class objects
```

```python
#Create an enemy object
class VampireSprite(sprite.Sprite):

    #Set up enemy instances
    def __init__(self):
        super().__init__()
        self.speed = 2
        self.lane = randint(0, 4)
        all_vampires.add(self)
        self.image = VAMPIRE_PIZZA.copy()
        y = 50 + self.lane * 100
        self.rect = self.image.get_rect(center = (1100, y))

    #Set up enemy movement
    def update(self, game_window):
        game_window.blit(self.image, (self.rect.x, self.rect.y))

#--------------------------------------------------
#Create class instances and groups

#Create a group for all the VampireSprite instances
all_vampires = sprite.Group()

#--------------------------------------------------
#Initialize and draw the background grid

#Define the color of the grid outline
tile_color = WHITE

#Populate the background grid
for row in range(6):
    for column in range(11):
        draw.rect(BACKGROUND, tile_color,
                (WIDTH * column, HEIGHT * row, WIDTH, HEIGHT), 1)

#Display the background image to the screen
GAME_WINDOW.blit(BACKGROUND, (0,0))

#--------------------------------------------------
#Game loop

#Define the conditions for running the loop
game_running = True

#Start game loop
while game_running:
```

```python
#----------------------
#Check for events

#Start loop to check for and handle events
for event in pygame.event.get():

    #Exit the loop when the game window closes
    if event.type == QUIT:
        game_running = False

#----------------------
#Spawn sprites

#Spawn vampire pizza sprites
if randint(1, SPAWN_RATE) == 1:
    VampireSprite()

#----------------------
#Update displays

#Update enemies
for vampire in all_vampires:
    vampire.update(GAME_WINDOW)

#Update all images on the screen
display.update()

#Close main game loop
#----------------------------------------------

#Clean up the game
pygame.quit()
```

Level Up!

0 1 2 3 4 5 6 7 8 9 10 11 12 13 ★

You've added sprites to your program by:
* Creating a new class
* Adding methods to the class
* Using the randint method to spawn sprites
* Using a for loop to update the sprite images

Stellar job!

Chapter 7
Moving the Pizzas

We've made the enemies (our vampire pizzas) appear on the screen. The next step is to get them to move along their rows to the pizza boxes on the other side of the screen.

To make this happen, we need to do two things:

1. Set the **frame rate** of the game.

2. Set up the movement rules for vampire pizzas.

Frame Rate

Frame rate in your game is the number of times per second that the game updates its buffer. Remember, to create the impression of movement, the program is drawing images to chunks of memory called buffer.

So a frame rate of **60fps** (or frames per second) would refresh **60** times within **1** second. Think back to our flipbook analogy (page 73).

The faster you flip the book, the smoother the movement appears. In general, a low frame rate will create jerky-looking movement. The higher the frame rate, the smoother the movement will appear.

Your computer screen also has its own frame rate. You will only control the frame rate of your game, but be aware that it can look different on different screens. Most screen frame rates are multiples of 30. If you choose a frame rate that is also a multiple of 30 for your games, your graphics will tend to look better.

Frame rate is important to video game design and digital animation. If you are interested in either of these topics, you should continue to build your skills and learn more about how computers render graphics.

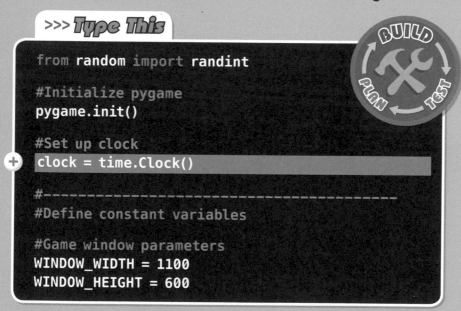

Set Up the Clock

To set up the frame rate of our game, we are going to use an object in Pygame called **Clock**. Pygame already created the Clock object for us. All we have to do is create an instance of Clock in our game.

>>> **Type This**

```
from random import randint

#Initialize pygame
pygame.init()

#Set up clock
clock = time.Clock()

#-----------------------------------------------
#Define constant variables

#Game window parameters
WINDOW_WIDTH = 1100
WINDOW_HEIGHT = 600
```

Now we have a clock in our game. This object will keep track of time and allow us to set the frame rate.

Let's create a constant variable that sets the frame rate to 60fps (frames per second). Later, when you customize the game, you can adjust the frame rate up or down by changing the value of this variable.

>>> Type This

```
WHITE = (255, 255, 255)

#Set up rates
SPAWN_RATE = 360
FRAME_RATE = 60

#--------------------------------------------------
#Load assets

#Create the game window
GAME_WINDOW = display.set_mode(WINDOW_RES)
display.set_caption('Attack of the Vampire Pizzas!')
```

We will add the frame rate to the game loop.

```
    for vampire in all_vampires:
        vampire.update(GAME_WINDOW)

    display.update()

#To Do: Set the frame rate here

#--------------------------------------------------
#Close main game loop

#Clean up the game
pygame.quit()
```

1. Call the method `tick` on the `clock` object.

2. Pass the `FRAME_RATE` as an argument.

Check Your Work

`clock.tick(FRAME_RATE)`

If you were to run your game right now, you wouldn't notice any changes. Right now the images we're using aren't moving anywhere, so refreshing the screen at a faster or slower rate won't affect how we see them.

Frame Rate and Speed

Frame rate is not the same thing as the speed that sprites move in your game, but the two concepts are connected. To understand how frame rate and speed work together, imagine two bikes: one with very small wheels, and one with very large wheels.

If the wheels both turn 10 times, the bike with the larger wheels will end up moving farther. This is because the larger wheels cover more distance than the smaller wheels, so the bike with larger wheels will make it to the end of the block first.

There are two ways to make a bike go faster:

Either increase the number of times per minute that the wheels turn

or

increase the size of the wheels.

Increasing the number of times per minute that the wheels turn is like increasing the frame rate. Increasing the size of the wheel is like increasing the number of pixels that a sprite changes its location per frame. For example, a vampire pizza moving at 2 pixels per frame appears to move faster than a vampire pizza moving at 1 pixel per frame.

Suppose all the vampire pizzas are moving at 1 pixel per frame. They will all appear to move slower if we change the frame rate from 120 times per second to 30 times per second.

You can adjust the speed of your sprites by programming them to change location by some number of pixels. However, if you need to adjust the overall speed of the game to make adjustments to how the images look or move, you will change the frame rate.

Enemy Movement

Now let's set up the rules for the movement of the vampire pizzas.

How do we want vampire pizzas to move?

1. Move from the right side of the screen to the left side

2. Move in one row only

3. Move at a constant speed (they should all move at the same speed without slowing down or speeding up partway across the screen)

Now that we are clear on the movement rules for vampire pizzas, let's modify the `update()` method in the `VampireSprite` class to include movement rules.

>>> **Type This**

```
#VampireSprite class, __init__ method
        y = 50 + self.lane * 100
        self.rect = self.image.get_rect(center=(1100, y))
#Create function that moves enemies from right
#to left and destroys them after they leave the screen
    def update(self, game_window):
#Erase the last sprite image
        game_window.blit(BACKGROUND,
                        (self.rect.x, self.rect.y), self.rect)
#Move the sprites
        self.rect.x -= self.speed
#Update the sprite image to the new location
        game_window.blit(self.image, (self.rect.x, self.rect.y))

game_running = True
while game_running:
```

Take a Closer Look

```
            y = 50 + self.lane * 100
            self.rect = self.image.get_rect(center=(1100, y))
#Create function that moves enemies from right
#to left and destroys them after they leave the screen
    def update(self, game_window):
#Erase the last sprite image
        game_window.blit(BACKGROUND,
                        (self.rect.x, self.rect.y), self.rect)
#Move the sprites
        self.rect.x -= self.speed
#Update the sprite image to the new location
        game_window.blit(self.image, (self.rect.x, self.rect.y))
```

`self.rect.x -= self.speed`

Remember, the sprites don't actually move. We are redrawing them at a new location each time the frame rate refreshes. Notice that we are actually telling the vampire pizza to change its x-coordinate by –2 each time the game loop runs. This means it will be redrawn 2 pixels to the left every time we call `update()`. This covers all of our movement rules:

1) move from right to left, 2) stay in one row, and
3) move at a constant speed.

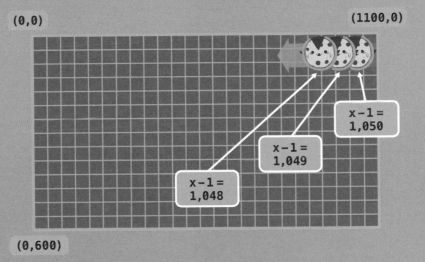

If you did not blit the background image over the the old sprite images, it would look like the vampire pizza is stretched across the row.

```
        y = 50 + self.lane * 100
        self.rect = self.image.get_rect(center=(1100, y))
#Create function that moves enemies from right
#to left and destroys them after they leave the screen
    def update(self, game_window):
#Erase the last sprite image
        game_window.blit(BACKGROUND,
                    (self.rect.x, self.rect.y), self.rect)

#Move the sprites
        self.rect.x -= self.speed
#Update the sprite image to the new location
        game_window.blit(self.image, (self.rect.x, self.rect.y))
```

`game_window.blit(BACKGROUND,`
`        (self.rect.x, self.rect.y), self.rect)`

This line of code erases each drawing as it is replaced. This will create movement. Let's see how it works:

This is the surface where we want to display our image.

This method displays images on the screen.

This argument tells the program what we want to display: the background image.

`game_window.blit(BACKGROUND,`
`        (self.rect.x, self.rect.y), self.rect)`

This argument tells the program where to display the image. We want to display the background image over the last location of the vampire sprite, so we give the vampire sprite's x and y coordinates as the location.

This argument tells the program what part of the image to display.

Usually we leave the last argument out and it displays the entire image. This time, we only want the piece of the background image that will cover the last location of the vampire sprite. `self.rect()` is the same thing as giving the area of just that sprite.

Level Up!

0 1 2 3 4 5 6 7 8 9 10 11 12 13 ★

You did it! Now every time we call `VampireSprite.update()` three things will happen:

1. The old VampireSprite instance will be erased by drawing the background image over the old location.

2. It will change the x-coordinate of the VampireSprite instance to create the impression of movement along a row.

3. It will draw the new VampireSprite instance in the updated location. When this runs very quickly, it will appear as if the sprite is moving smoothly across the screen. Let's try it out!

Check Your Work

Run your program to check your work. You should see vampire pizzas moving across the screen from right to left. Programs run from top to bottom, but they don't get written that way. Check the order of your code carefully.

TEST
BUILD
PLAN

```
from random import randint

#Initialize pygame
pygame.init()

#Set up the clock
clock = time.Clock()

#-----------------------------------------------
#Define constant variables

#Define the parameters of the game window
WINDOW_WIDTH = 1100
WINDOW_HEIGHT = 600
```

```
WHITE = (255, 255, 255)

#Set up rates
SPAWN_RATE = 360
FRAME_RATE = 60


#--------------------------------------------------
#Load assets

#Create the game window
GAME_WINDOW = display.set_mode(WINDOW_RES)
```

```
#VampireSprite class, __init__ method
        self.image = VAMPIRE_PIZZA.copy()
        y = 50 + self.lane * 100
        self.rect = self.image.get_rect(center = (1100, y))

    #Set up enemy movement
    def update(self, game_window):
        game_window.blit(BACKGROUND,
                            (self.rect.x, self.rect.y), self.rect)
        self.rect.x -= self.speed
        game_window.blit(self.image, (self.rect.x, self.rect.y))

#--------------------------------------------------
#Create class instances and groups

#Create a sprite group for all VampireSprite instances
all_vampires = sprite.Group()
```

```
    #Update all images on the screen
    display.update()

    #Set the frame rate
    clock.tick(FRAME_RATE)


#--------------------------------------------------
#Close main game loop

#Clean up the game
pygame.quit()
```

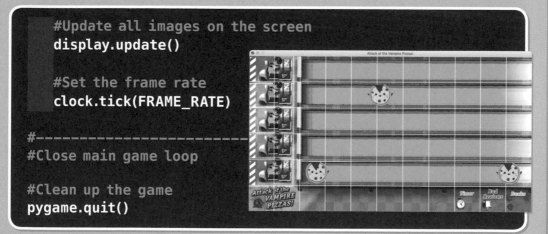

Chapter 8

Interactive Fields

We've got the enemies moving. Now we need to be able to stop them!

We want to interact with the vampire pizzas by laying down different types of traps. Each trap will cover one tile of the background grid.

To do this, we need to make our program do two things:

1. Make it so the player can interact with the background grid by selecting tiles where they lay down traps.

2. Make it so the vampire pizzas can detect when they hit a trap and respond to the effect of the trap.

First we'll make the grid tiles respond to mouse clicks. Then we'll make the vampire pizzas respond to tiles.

The Invisible Grid

We need to overlay our background grid with a grid of **Rect objects**. In Pygame, **Rect objects** are invisible rectangles that can be attached to any surface and that can interact with one another. For example, Rects can sense when they come into contact with another Rect. This is called **collision detection**.

First we'll create a new class of objects. These objects will be our interactive background tiles. Let's call the class `BackgroundTiles`. We'll base this new object on the rules for all Sprite objects in Pygame.

▶ **Your Turn**

```
#VampireSprite class, update method
    def update(self, game_window):
        game_window.blit(BACKGROUND,
                        (self.rect.x, self.rect.y), self.rect)
        self.rect.x -= self.speed
        game_window.blit(self.image, (self.rect.x, self.rect.y))

#Create a class of background tile sprites
#To Do: Create BackgroundTile class here
#To Do: Define init method here
#To Do: Use super method here
#To Do: Set effect attribute here
#To Do: Set rect attribute here
#-------------------------------------------------
#Create class instances and groups
all_vampires = sprite.Group()
#-------------------------------------------------
#Initialize and draw the background grid

tile_color = WHITE
for row in range(6):
```

1. Create a subclass called `BackgroundTile` based on the `sprite.Sprite` base class.

2. Define an `__init__` method for BackgroundTile. Give it two arguments, `self` and `rect`.

3. Use the `super()` method to bring the set-up rules for the base class into your `__init__()` method.

4. Create an attribute for `self` called `effect`. Assign it the value `False`.

Power Up: Use the VampireSprite class in your code as a model for creating classes and defining init methods.

5. Create an attribute for `self` called `rect`. Assign it the value `rect`.

```python
class BackgroundTile(sprite.Sprite):

    def __init__(self, rect):
        super().__init__()
        self.effect = False
        self.rect = rect
```

Take a Closer Look

```python
#Create a class of background tiles
class BackgroundTile(sprite.Sprite):

    def __init__(self, rect):
        super().__init__()
        self.effect = False
        self.rect = rect

#------------------------------
#Create class instances
```

`self.effect = False`

We just created the attribute `effect` and gave it the value `False`. As the programmer, you know that `effect` represents whether or not a background tile has had a trap applied to it, but the program only knows this as a name that stores a **boolean** (True or False) value.

Ideas for Programmers

A `list` is a data type. Items in the list are separated by commas and surrounded by square brackets. The order of the items in a list matters. So a list of weapons that stop vampire pizzas would be:

This list is stored in a variable named `weapons`.

These are the items in the list.

The items in the list are surrounded by square brackets.

```python
weapons = ['garlic', 'wooden pizza cutters',
           'pizza box with a sun roof']
```

Unlike tuples, you can change the order of the list and the number of items in it.

Now that we have created a sprite class that contains each interactive tile, we can overlay these new "invisible" sprite tiles onto the background grid that we drew earlier.

>>> Type This

```python
#Create a group for all VampireSprite instances
all_vampires = sprite.Group()
#-------------------------------------------------
#Initialize and draw the background grid

#Create an empty list
tile_grid = []
tile_color = WHITE
for row in range(6):
#Create an empty list each time the loop runs
    row_of_tiles = []
#Add each of the six lists called row_of_tiles to the
#tile_grid list above.
    tile_grid.append(row_of_tiles)
    for column in range(11):
#Create an invisible rect for each background tile sprite
        tile_rect = Rect(WIDTH * column, HEIGHT * row,
                        WIDTH, HEIGHT)
#For each column in each row, create a new background tile sprite
        new_tile = BackgroundTile(tile_rect)
#Add each new background tile sprite to the correct
#row_of_tiles list
        row_of_tiles.append(new_tile)
#Draw the visible tiles
        draw.rect(BACKGROUND, tile_color, (WIDTH * column,
                HEIGHT * row, WIDTH, HEIGHT), 1)

GAME_WINDOW.blit(BACKGROUND, (0,0))
```

Take a Closer Look

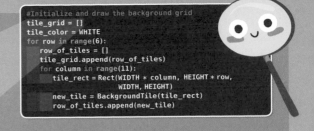

```
#Initialize and draw the background grid
tile_grid = []
tile_color = WHITE
for row in range(6):
    row_of_tiles = []
    tile_grid.append(row_of_tiles)
    for column in range(11):
        tile_rect = Rect(WIDTH * column, HEIGHT * row,
                         WIDTH, HEIGHT)
        new_tile = BackgroundTile(tile_rect)
        row_of_tiles.append(new_tile)
```

```
tile_grid = []
```

Empty List: There are no items inside the square brackets. This is because we will add the items to the list later. As each new background tile is created in the loop, it will be added as an item to this list.

```
for row in range(6):
    row_of_tiles = []
    tile_grid.append(row_of_tiles)
```

List of Lists: We are creating six more empty lists, one for each time the loop runs. Each new empty list is added to the list called `tile_grid`. The method `append` adds new items to the lists. Now `tile_grid` is a list of empty lists.

You can imagine it like this:

tile_grid = [[], [], [], [], [], []]

```
for column in range(11):
    tile_rect = Rect(WIDTH * column, HEIGHT * row,
                     WIDTH, HEIGHT)
    new_tile = BackgroundTile(tile_rect)
    row_of_tiles.append(new_tile)
```

Fill the Lists: Each new background tile is added to a `row_of_tiles` list, every time the loop runs. You can imagine each `row_of_tiles` list like this:

Row_of_tiles = [new_tile, new_tile, new_tile, new_tile, new_tile, new_tile, new_tile, new_tile, new_tile, new_tile, new_tile]

This will add eleven background tiles to each of the six lists. That's how we get a grid with eleven columns and six rows!

Now let's revisit our `tile_grid` list. This is a special kind of list called a two-dimensional array.

A **two-dimensional array** is a *list of lists*. `tile_grid` will have 6 lists of 11 items. We can't see the lists laid out in the code because they're stored in the computer's memory. Let's imagine that instead of six lists of eleven `new_tile` sprites, we have a two-dimensional array that is storing six lists of eleven oddly cheerful pizza slice emojis each. Here's what that would look like:

pizza_grid = [

[🍕, 🍕, 🍕, 🍕, 🍕, 🍕, 🍕, 🍕, 🍕, 🍕, 🍕],
[🍕, 🍕, 🍕, 🍕, 🍕, 🍕, 🍕, 🍕, 🍕, 🍕, 🍕],
[🍕, 🍕, 🍕, 🍕, 🍕, 🍕, 🍕, 🍕, 🍕, 🍕, 🍕],
[🍕, 🍕, 🍕, 🍕, 🍕, 🍕, 🍕, 🍕, 🍕, 🍕, 🍕],
[🍕, 🍕, 🍕, 🍕, 🍕, 🍕, 🍕, 🍕, 🍕, 🍕, 🍕],
[🍕, 🍕, 🍕, 🍕, 🍕, 🍕, 🍕, 🍕, 🍕, 🍕, 🍕],

]

Can you see how this type of list is helpful for storing the tile sprites that make up our background grid?

Indexing

An **index** is the position of a value in a list. Let's look at an example:

animals =

    0   1   2   3   4

Wait a second! There are five animals in our list! Why do the numbers only go up to four?

Remember: Computers start counting at zero. So there are five items, numbered **0–4**.

These numbers are called the **index** of each list value.

So the index of is **2**.

Let's look at the pattern for using an index in our program:

```
lion = animals[0]
```

Take a look at our list. We just stored in the variable `lion`.

How would we use an index to create a variable for •••• ?

```
unicorn = animals[3]
```

Make the Grid Interactive

Let's add the ability for the player to interact with the grid by clicking on it with the mouse.

An **event** "listens" for a certain action to happen, like a mouse click. It "hears" when the action happens and runs a block of code in response. Pygame has a built-in event for exactly this. We just need to use the correct name for the event and add the code block that we would like to run in response. In Pygame, this event is called **MOUSEBUTTONDOWN**.

```
#Check for and handle events
    for event in pygame.event.get():
#Exit the loop when the game window closes
        if event.type == QUIT:
            running = False
#Listen for the mouse button to be clicked and run when clicked
        elif event.type == MOUSEBUTTONDOWN:
#Get the (x,y) coordinate where the mouse was clicked
#on the screen
            coordinates = mouse.get_pos()
            x = coordinates[0]
            y = coordinates[1]
#Find the background tile at the location where the mouse
#was clicked and change the value of effect to True
            tile_y = y // 100
            tile_x = x // 100
            tile_grid[tile_y][tile_x].effect = True

#-------------------------------------------------
#Spawn vampire pizza sprites
    if randint(1, SPAWN_RATE) == 1:
        VampireSprite()
```

*Remember, effect can be either True or False.
When it is False, there is no effect
placed on that tile. When it is
set to True, it means that
some type of trap has been
placed on the tile.*

Now when the player clicks on a tile, they will be able to lay a trap.

Take a Closer Look

Let's look at an example. If a player clicks on the screen at coordinates (500,400) this is what would happen:

```
x = 500        tile_x = 500//100  →  5
y = 400        tile_y = 400//100  →  4
```

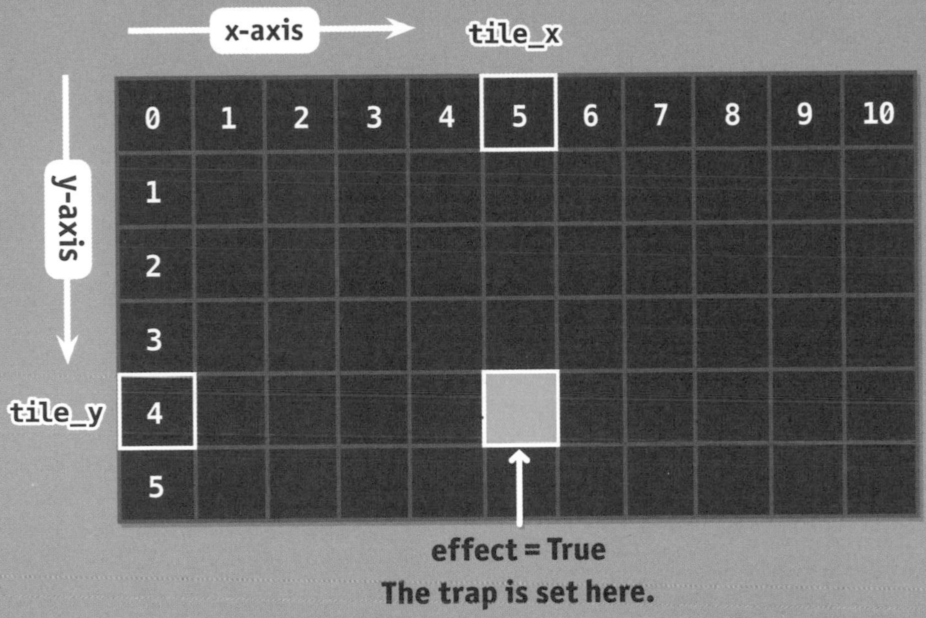

x-axis →   tile_x

	0	1	2	3	4	**5**	6	7	8	9	10
1											
2											
3											
4											
5											

y-axis ↓

tile_y → **4**

effect = True
The trap is set here.

Test It Out

We need to test out our new code to see if it detects when the player clicks on the screen. We're not quite ready to add a trap, so we can test it with print statements instead.

When someone clicks on the screen, let's have it print the **x, y** coordinates where the click happened and the sentence **"You clicked me!"**

```
            tile_y = y // 100
            tile_x = x // 100
            tile_grid[tile_y][tile_x].effect=True
            print(x,y)
#To Do: Add second print statement here

#————————————————————————————————————————
#Spawn vampire pizzas
    if randint(1, SPAWN_RATE) == 1:
        VampireSprite()
```

▶ **Your Turn**

1. Now it's your turn. Add a new `print` statement with the sentence `'You clicked me!'`

Don't forget that it's a string, so it needs to be surrounded in quotes.

2. Run your code and click on the screen in three different places.

Take a look at the terminal. You should see a readout that looks similar to this:

```
● ● ●         vampire_pizza_directory— -bash—100x10
User—Mac:~ Users/Hedgie/vampire_pizza_directory/python
VampirePizzaAttack.py
538 249
You clicked me!
941 59
You clicked me!
334 461
You clicked me!
```

If you get an error or don't see either a set of coordinates or the string `'You clicked me!'`, then stop and debug.

Grace's Corner

Print Statements

Print statements are very useful for programmers, because they make some of the things that happen "behind the scenes" in our program visible.

You can quickly test to see if a new feature is working just like we did with detecting mouse clicks. You can also use print statements to debug if your program is running but not working correctly.

For example, if my vampire pizzas were only spawning within the top two rows, this would be a bug, because they are meant to spawn into *all* of the rows at random. I could find the place in my program where the rows are selected and print the row number each time a pizza is spawned.

```python
def __init__(self, rect):
    super().__init__()
    self.speed = 2
    self.lane = randint(0, 4)
    all_vampires.add(self)
    self.image = VAMPIRE_PIZZA.copy()
    y = 50 + self.lane * 10
    self.rect = self.image.get_rect(center=(1100, y))
    print(y)
```

If our code is correct, we should get values for y that are **50, 150, 250, 350, 450,** or **550.** If we get anything else, we have found the bug.

If we ran this code, we would get the following values: **50, 60, 70, 80, 90,** or **100.** We would know that the error is somewhere in the `__init__` method. Can you spot the bug?

Next time you run into a bug, see what you can make visible in the program. Try adding a print statement. Then run your code and check the terminal. Use the information that you get from the terminal to fix your code. Don't forget to delete the print statements or turn them into a comment after you are done debugging.

Check Your Work

Run your code to check your work. Make sure that you click on the screen to test the interactive part of your game file.

```python
    #Set up enemy movement
    def update(self, game_window):
        game_window.blit(BACKGROUND,
                        (self.rect.x, self.rect.y), self.rect)
        self.rect.x -= self.speed
        game_window.blit(self.image, (self.rect.x, self.rect.y))

#Create a background tile object
class BackgroundTile(sprite.Sprite):

#Set up instances of background tiles
    def __init__(self, rect):
        super().__init__()
        self.effect = False
        self.rect = rect
#------------------------------------------------
#Create class instances and groups

#Create a group for all VampireSprite instances
all_vampires = sprite.Group()

#------------------------------------------------
#Initialize and draw the background grid

#Create empty list to hold tile grid
tile_grid = []
#Define the color of the grid outline
tile_color = WHITE

#Populate the background grid
for row in range(6):
    row_of_tiles = []
    tile_grid.append(row_of_tiles)
    for column in range(11):
        tile_rect = Rect(WIDTH * column, HEIGHT * row,
                        WIDTH, HEIGHT)
        new_tile = BackgroundTile(tile_rect)
        row_of_tiles.append(new_tile)
        draw.rect(BACKGROUND, tile_color, (WIDTH * column,
                HEIGHT * row, WIDTH, HEIGHT), 1)

#Display the background image to the screen
GAME_WINDOW.blit(BACKGROUND, (0,0))
```

```python
#Start loop to check for and handle events
for event in pygame.event.get():

    #Exit the loop when the game window closes
    if event.type == QUIT:
        game_running = False

    #Set up the background tiles to respond to mouse clicks
    elif event.type == MOUSEBUTTONDOWN:
        coordinates = mouse.get_pos()
        x = coordinates[0]
        y = coordinates[1]
        tile_y = y // 100
        tile_x = x // 100
        tile_grid[tile_y][tile_x].effect = True
        print(x, y)
        print('You clicked me!')

#-------------------------------------------------------
#Spawn sprites

    #Spawn vampire pizza sprites
    if randint(1, SPAWN_RATE) == 1:
        VampireSprite()
```

Level Up!

0 1 2 3 4 5 6 7 8 9 10 11 12 13 ★

Great! You used a two-dimensional array and an event to make your background grid interactive. You also used print statements to test your code.

Chapter 9

Collision Detection

In the last chapter, we tested the mouse-click event by printing strings. But instead of printing strings, we actually want the player to be able to set traps when they click on the tiles. You can go into your code and delete the print statements we used to test our code in Chapter 8.

>>> Type This

```
        tile_y = y // 100
        tile_x = x // 100
        tile_grid[tile_y][tile_x].effect = True
    print(x, y)
    print('You clicked me!')

#------------------------------------------------
#Spawn vampire pizzas

    if randint(1, SPAWN_RATE) == 1:
        VampireSprite()
```

For the traps to work, we need:

1. The vampire pizza sprites to know when they touch a trap

2. To have the trap affect the vampire pizza sprite

To do this, we will set up a series of tests using **if** statements.

Let's create a slowdown trap for our vampire pizzas that will result in—you guessed it—their slowing. But how will the program know when the vampire pizza has come into contact with the trap? In order to tell the program when two things collide, we need to add **collision detection**. But first, we need to learn about **conditionals**.

Ideas for Programmers

Conditionals

A **conditional** tests if a certain statement is True, and runs a block of code if it IS True.

Let's look at an example:

```
x = 1
if x == 1:
    print('True')
```

In this example, we see that x equals 1. The conditional says that **IF x does equal 1**, then the program should print the string, "**True**." But why are there two equal signs in the conditional statement? In Python, when we assign a value to a variable, like **x = 1**, we use one equal sign. But when we test to see if something is equal, we use two equal signs.

Remember: One equal sign assigns value. Two equal signs ask the question: *Are these equal?*

So what would happen if we ran the code above? Since **1 == 1** is True, the code would print '**True**.'

And what would happen if the code was written like this?

```
x = 2
if x == 1:
    print('True')
```

Nothing would happen, because this code only runs if the conditional statement is True. **2 == 1** is False, so the print statement would not run.

We could also run code when the conditional statement is **NOT** True. For example:

```
x = ?
if x == 2:
    print('True')
else:
    print('False')
```

In this example, if x equals 2, the program will print "**True.**" If x equals *any other number*, the program will print "**False.**" Else means "**if not.**"

If a variable stores a boolean value (**True** or **False**), then the program automatically tests if it is **True.** In the following example, when a player meets the **win** condition of a game, the value of the variable win is changed to **True:**

```
win = True
if win:
    print('True')
else:
    print('False')
```

Notice that the line of code

```
if win:
```

actually means "if the value of **win** is **True.**"

We can test for other things, too:

Symbol	Meaning	True Examples
==	Are these values **equal**?	`if 1 == 1:`
!=	Are these values **not equal**?	`if 2 != 1:`
>	Is the first value **greater than** the other value?	`if 3 > 1:`
<	Is the first value **less than** the other value?	`if 1 < 3:`
>=	Is the first value **greater than or equal to** the other value?	`if 3 >= 3:`
<=	Is the first value **less than or equal to** the other value?	`if 3 <= 4:`

Now that we've learned about conditionals, let's get back to collision detection.

We'll set up collision detection inside the game loop. Every time the game loop runs, it will test each of the vampire pizzas to see if it has touched a tile with a slowdown trap on it.

BUILD
PLAN · TEST

```
#Spawn vampire pizza sprites
    if randint(1, SPAWN_RATE) == 1:
        VampireSprite()


#-------------------------------------------------
#Set up collision detection
#Run through each vampire pizza sprite in the
#list all_vampires
    for vampire in all_vampires:
#Store the row where the vampire sprite is located
        tile_row = tile_grid[vampire.rect.y // 100]
#Store the current location of the left edge of the
#vampire sprite
        vamp_left_side = vampire.rect.x // 100
#Store the current location of the right edge of the
#vampire sprite
        vamp_right_side = (vampire.rect.x +
                        vampire.rect.width) // 100
#If the vampire sprite is on the grid, find which column
#it is in
        if 0 <= vamp_left_side <= 10:
            left_tile = tile_row[vamp_left_side]
#Return no column if the vampire sprite is not on the grid
        else:
            left_tile = None
#To Do: Test if the right side of the vampire sprite is
#on the grid
#To Do: Store the location of right_tile
#To Do: Test if the right side of the vampire sprite
#is not on the screen
#To Do: Set the value of right_tile to None


#-------------------------------------------------
#Update displays
    for vampire in all_vampires:
        vampire.update(GAME_WINDOW)

    display.update()
```

Take a Closer Look

```
#Set up collision detection
    for vampire in all_vampires:
        tile_row = tile_grid[vampire.rect.y // 100]
        vamp_left_side = vampire.rect.x // 100
        vamp_right_side = (vampire.rect.x +
                           vampire.rect.width) // 100
        if 0 <= vamp_left_side <= 10:
            left_tile = tile_row[vamp_left_side]
#Return no column if the vampire sprite is not on the grid
        else:
            left_tile = None
```

```
tile_row = tile_grid[vampire.rect.y // 100]
```

How does the program know which row the vampire pizza is in? The two-dimensional array called `tile_grid` stores the data that creates the background grid. You can imagine it like this:

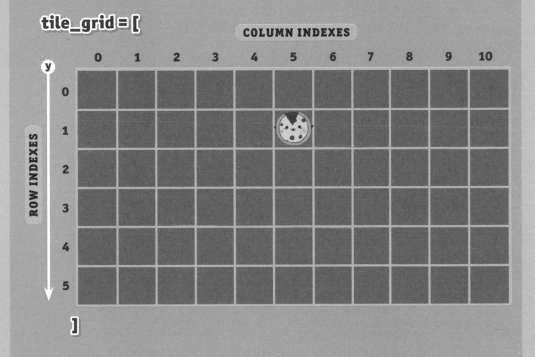

tile_grid = [

COLUMN INDEXES

ROW INDEXES

]

In the grid above, the pizza has a y-coordinate of **150**. The program takes the y-coordinate of the vampire pizza, and divides that number by **100**.

If we divide **150** by **100**, we get **1.5**. For our purposes, we only care about the whole number, which tells us the index of the row is **1**.

tile_row = tile_grid [1]

tile_row = 1

0 1 2 3 4 5 6 7 8 9 10

```
#Set up collision detection
for vampire in all_vampires:
    tile_row = tile_grid[vampire.rect.y // 100]
    vamp_left_side = vampire.rect.x // 100
    vamp_right_side = (vampire.rect.x +
                       vampire.rect.width) // 100
    if 0 <= vamp_left_side <= 10:
        left_tile = tile_row[vamp_left_side]
#Returns no column if the vampire sprite is not on the grid
    else:
        left_tile = None
```

```
vamp_left_side = vampire.rect.x // 100
vamp_right_side = (vampire.rect.x +
    vampire.rect.width) // 100
```

To explain how this code finds the two sides of the vampire pizza, let's look at the image below.

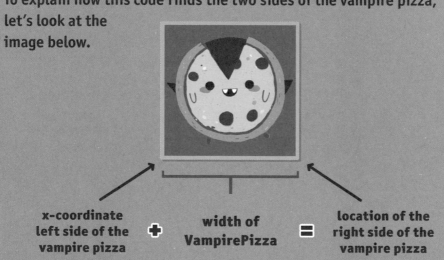

x-coordinate
left side of the
vampire pizza

+

width of
VampirePizza

=

location of the
right side of the
vampire pizza

The value of the x-coordinate (divided by **100**) is the left side of the vampire pizza.

To find the value of the right side, we use what we know. We take the value of the left wall, add the width of the pizza, and end up on the right side. Let's return to the code.

Look at the test that locates the left side of the
vampire pizza sprite. Use this code as a model to add
a test that locates the right side of the vampire pizza.

1. Test if `vamp_right_side` is greater than or equal to `0` and less
than or equal to `10`.

2. If the test is **True**, create a variable called `right_tile` that
stores the location of the right side of the vampire pizza.
Use `vamp_right_side` as the index of `tile_row`.

3. If the test is not **True**, change the value of `right_tile` to `None`.

You can check your work at the end of the chapter.

Take a Closer Look

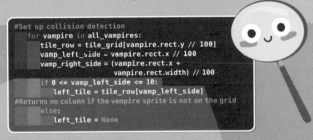

```python
#Set up collision detection
    for vampire in all_vampires:
        tile_row = tile_grid[vampire.rect.y // 100]
        vamp_left_side = vampire.rect.x // 100
        vamp_right_side = (vampire.rect.x +
                           vampire.rect.width) // 100
        if 0 <= vamp_left_side <= 10:
            left_tile = tile_row[vamp_left_side]
#Returns no column if the vampire sprite is not on the grid
        else:
            left_tile = None
```

```python
if 0 <= vamp_left_side <=10:
    left_tile = tile_row[vamp_left_side]
else:
    left_tile = None
```

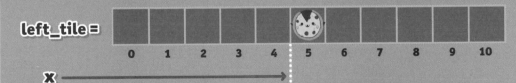

left_tile =

| 0 | 1 | 2 | 3 | 4 | 5 | 6 | 7 | 8 | 9 | 10 |

x ⟶

Now we want to test if the value of `vamp_left_side` is between
0 and **10**. If this is **False**, then it's outside the game window.
If it's **True**, then we'll create a new variable called `left_tile`.
The value of `left_tile` will be the index of the tile that the
vampire is touching with its left side.

right_tile =

```
0   1   2   3   4   5   6   7   8   9   10
```

X →

We will also test if the value of `vamp_right_side` is between **0** and **10**. If this is **False**, then it's outside the game window. If it's **True**, then we'll create a new variable called `right_tile`. The value of `right_tile` will be the index of the tile that the vampire is touching with its right side.

Ideas for Programmers

Complex If Statements

Sometimes **if** statements have more than one condition. For example, let's say that we only want to eat between **2** and **4** slices of pizza. We could write an if statement like this:

```
if slices > 1 and slices <= 4:
    slices.eat()
```

If the number of slices is **1** or less, the test will be **False**. It will stop and not test to see if the slices are less than or equal to 4.

We could write the same test in a **nested if statement**:

```
if slices > 1:
    if slices <= 4:
        slices.eat()
```

The order that you test conditions in complex or nested if statements can improve the efficiency of your code.

We've finally located our vampire pizza on the grid, and we know which background tiles it's touching. Let's return to our code.

>>> Type This

```
        if 0 <= vamp_right_side <= 10:
            right_tile = tile_row[vamp_right_side]
#Returns no column if the vampire sprite is not on the grid
        else:
            right_tile = None


#Test if the left side of the vampire pizza is touching
#a tile and if that tile has been clicked.
#If true, change the vampire speed to 1.
        if bool(left_tile) and left_tile.effect:
            vampire.speed = 1
#Test if the right side of the sprite is touching a tile
#and if that tile has been clicked
        if bool(right_tile) and right_tile.effect:
#Test if the right and left sides of the sprite are
#touching different tiles
            if right_tile != left_tile:
#If both tests are true, change the vampire speed to 1
                vampire.speed = 1
#Delete the vampire sprite when it leaves the screen
        if vampire.rect.x <= 0:
            vampire.kill()
```

Take a Closer Look

```
if bool (left_tile) and left_tile.effect:
    vampire.speed = 1
if bool(right_tile) and right_tile.effect:
    if right_tile != left_tile:
        vampire.speed = 1
if vampire.rect.x <= 0:
    vampire.kill()
```

```
if bool(right_tile) and right_tile.effect:
    if right_tile != left_tile:
        vampire.speed = 1
```

`if bool(right_tile):` tests if the right edge of the vampire pizza sprite is touching a tile. If it is, the test returns **True**. If it's not touching a tile on the grid, the test returns **False**. True/False is a boolean data type. This test would work if we used `if right_tile:`, but we're using the `bool` function for clarity.

Here we are testing if the right edge of the vampire pizza is touching a tile *and* if that tile has been clicked. Only if the first test is **True**, the program will test if both sides of the vampire pizza are touching the same tile. This will make sure the trap effect is only applied once.

Let's create variables to store the different speed settings.

```
SPAWN_RATE = 360
FRAME_RATE = 60
#Define speeds
REG_SPEED = 2
#To Do: Add the variable for slow speed here

#----------------------------------------------
#Load assets

#Create the game window
GAME_WINDOW = display.set_mode(WINDOW_RES)
display.set_caption('Attack of the Vampire Pizzas!')
```

1. Type `REG_SPEED = 2` as shown.

2. Create a `SLOW_SPEED` variable and set the value to `1`.

Now you need to swap out the hard-coded integers for the new variable names.

```python
#VampireSprite class
    def __init__(self):
        super().__init__()
        self.speed = 2
        self.speed = REG_SPEED
        self.lane = randint(0, 4)
        all_vampires.add(self)
        self.image = VAMPIRE_PIZZA.copy()
```

3. Change the value of `self.speed` as shown.

```python
        self.speed = REG_SPEED
```

```python
        else:
            left_tile = None
        if bool(left_tile) and left_tile.effect:
            vampire.speed = 1
#To Do: Replace the value of vampire.speed
        if bool(right_tile) and right_tile.effect:
            if right_tile != left_tile:
                vampire.speed = 1
#To Do: Replace the value of vampire.speed
        if vampire.rect.x <= 0:
            vampire.kill()
```

4. Change both lines of code with the **speed** attribute using the variable `SLOW_SPEED`.

Commenting Out Code

When you get an error message, there is usually a line number in the message.

```
                          ⬆ User—-bash— 90×24
VampirePizzaAttack User—Mac:~ User$ python3 vampirepizza.py
  File "vampirepizza—error.py", line 172
    if vampire.rect.x <= 0
                       ^
SyntaxError: invalid syntax
VampirePizzaAttack user$ ▮
```

Sometimes the bug isn't actually on that line number but is instead somewhere near it. If you can't figure out where an error is, you can **comment out** lines of code to narrow down the possibilities. Commenting out code means that you add a **#** symbol in front of the line of code to temporarily make it into a comment.

If you knew that there was an error somewhere in the following code, you could comment out one part, then run the code. If you stop getting the error, you know that the part of the code that you commented out was causing the error message.

If you still got an error message, then you would try commenting out the next part of the code, and repeat that process until the code runs.

In this example, our game ran after we commented out the third if statement, so we would know that the error is somewhere in those two lines of code.

```
for vampire in all_vampires:
    if bool(left_tile) and left_tile.effect:
        vampire.speed = SLOW_SPEED
    if bool(right_tile) and right_tile.effect:
        if right_tile != left_tile:
            vampire.speed = SLOW_SPEED
    #if vampire.rect.x <= 0
        #vampire.kill()
```

Can you find it?

Check Your Work

Run your code to check your work. Click on some tiles. The vampire pizzas should slow down after touching the tiles that you clicked. If your program works differently, stop and debug.

```
#Set up rates
SPAWN_RATE = 360
FRAME_RATE = 60

#Define speeds
REG_SPEED = 2
SLOW_SPEED = 1

#----------------------------------------
#Load assets

#Create the game window
GAME_WINDOW = display.set_mode(WINDOW_RES)
display.set_caption('Attack of the Vampire Pizzas!')
```

```python
#Create an enemy object
class VampireSprite(sprite.Sprite):

    #Set up enemy instances
    def __init__(self):
        super().__init__()
        self.speed = REG_SPEED
        self.lane = randint(0, 4)
        all_vampires.add(self)
        self.image = VAMPIRE_PIZZA.copy()
        y = 50 + self.lane * 100
        self.rect = self.image.get_rect(center=(1100, y))
```

```python
    #Spawn vampire pizza sprites
    if randint(1, SPAWN_RATE) == 1:
        VampireSprite()

    #-----------------------
    #Set up collision detection

    #Set up detection for collision with background tiles
    for vampire in all_vampires:
        tile_row = tile_grid[vampire.rect.y // 100]
        vamp_left_side = vampire.rect.x // 100
        vamp_right_side = (vampire.rect.x +
                            vampire.rect.width) // 100
        if 0 <= vamp_left_side <= 10:
            left_tile = tile_row[vamp_left_side]
        else:
            left_tile = None
        if 0 <= vamp_right_side <= 10:
            right_tile = tile_row[vamp_right_side]
        else:
            right_tile = None
        if bool(left_tile) and left_tile.effect:
            vampire.speed = SLOW_SPEED
        if bool(right_tile) and right_tile.effect:
            if right_tile != left_tile:
                vampire.speed = SLOW_SPEED
        if vampire.rect.x <= 0:
            vampire.kill()
```

```
#----------------------
#Update displays

#Update enemies
for vampire in all_vampires:
    vampire.update(GAME_WINDOW)

#Update all images on the screen
display.update()
```

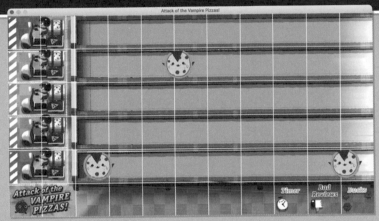

Level Up!

0 1 2 3 4 5 6 7 8 9 10 11 12 13 ★

Wow!!! You used complex conditional statements to test for which background tile a vampire pizza sprite is touching. You used conditionals to activate traps when they have been set by the player and when a vampire pizza touches them. Now you have a working trap in your game!

Chapter 10

Adding Points over Time

In our game, the player will need to prevent all of the vampire pizzas from reaching the pizza boxes for a certain amount of time. The player will do this by laying down traps that they can purchase using **pizza bucks**. Pizza bucks are a form of points that are earned over time.

In this chapter, you will lay the groundwork for your pizza-bucks economy. Before we can create the system of exchanging pizza bucks for traps, we will need to set up the point system.

We can decompose the point system into three parts:

1. **Keep track of how much time is passing in the game.**

2. **Add points (pizza bucks) at a set rate over time.**

3. **Display the points (pizza bucks) so that the player knows how many are available.**

First we'll create a class called **counters**. We'll add methods that will count game loops, add pizza bucks at a set rate, and display the amount of available pizza bucks to the player. Later on, we'll add other counters that we need.

>>> **Type This**

```
#VampireSprite class
    def update(self, game_window):
        game_window.blit(BACKGROUND,
                        (self.rect.x, self.rect.y), self.rect)

        self.rect.x -= self.speed
        game_window.blit(self.image, (self.rect.x, self.rect.y))


#Create new class
class Counters(object):
#Set up init method with four arguments
    def __init__(self, pizza_bucks, buck_rate, buck_booster):
#Start the game loop counter at 0
        self.loop_count = 0
#Set up the look of the counter on the screen
        self.display_font = font.Font('pizza_font.ttf', 25)
#Define the pizza_bucks attribute using the pizza_bucks
#argument
        self.pizza_bucks = pizza_bucks
#Define the buck_rate attribute using the buck_rate argument
        self.buck_rate = buck_rate
#To Do: Define the buck_booster attribute
#To Do: Define the bucks_rect attribute

class BackgroundTile(sprite.Sprite):
    def __init__(self):
        super().__init__()
```

Take a Closer Look

```
class Counters(object):
    def __init__(self, pizza_bucks, buck_rate, buck_booster):
        self.loop_count = 0
        self.display_font = font.Font('pizza_font.ttf', 25)
        self.pizza_bucks = pizza_bucks
        self.buck_rate = buck_rate
```

`def __init__(self, pizza_bucks, buck_rate, buck_booster):`

The `__init__` method will set up all the counters at the start of the game. We are passing it three arguments other than the special `self` argument.

The argument `pizza_bucks` will be the total number of **pizza_bucks** the player has at any time.

The `buck_rate` will set how often players earn **pizza_bucks**.

The `buck_booster` will indicate how many **pizza_bucks** players earn at a time.

```
class Counters(object):
    def __init__(self, pizza_bucks, buck_rate, buck_booster):
        self.loop_count = 0
        self.display_font = font.Font('pizza_font.ttf', 25)
        self.pizza_bucks = pizza_bucks
        self.buck_rate = buck_rate
```

`self.pizza_bucks = pizza_bucks`

Here, we are creating a new attribute called `self.pizza_bucks`. We are assigning it the value of whatever number is passed in with the argument `pizza_bucks`.

Your Turn

Look at the pattern we used for setting up attributes in the init method:

self.new_attribute = value

Use this pattern to set up two more attributes:

1. Set up an attribute called `buck_booster`. Use the argument `buck_booster` as the value.

2. Set up an attribute called `bucks_rect`. Use the value `None`.

We've set up our **Counters** class. Now we need to write some methods that will meet our three goals: keep track of time passing, add points over time at a set rate, and display the points to the player.

Set Up Instances of Counters

First we need to add some setup information.

>>> Type This

```
#Set up rates
SPAWN_RATE = 360
FRAME_RATE = 60
#Store the number of pizza bucks that players get at
#the start of the game
STARTING_BUCKS = 15
#To Do: Add BUCK_RATE here
#To Do: Add STARTING_BUCK_BOOSTER here

#Define speeds
REG_SPEED = 2
SLOW_SPEED = 1
```

1. `BUCK_RATE` will store the number of game loops that should run for the player to earn pizza bucks. Set the value to `120`.

2. `STARTING_BUCK_BOOSTER` will store the number of pizza bucks the player should earn each time the set amount of game loops runs. This variable stores the number that pizza bucks will increase by at the start of the game. Set the value to `1`.

Classes don't just run on their own. We need to create instances. Let's set up the instance of counters before we add any more methods to it.

 **Type This**

```
#---------------------------------------------
#Create class instances
all_vampires = sprite.Group()

counters = Counters(STARTING_BUCKS, BUCK_RATE,
                    STARTING_BUCK_BOOSTER)

#---------------------------------------------
#Initialize and draw the background grid

tile_grid = []
tile_color = WHITE
for row in range(6):
```

Take a Closer Look

The `Counters()` instance is stored in a variable called `counters`.

Take a look at the required arguments from the `__init__` method:

```
    def __init__(self, pizza_bucks, buck_rate, buck_booster):
```

We ignore self and use the variables that we just created to pass in the other information.

```
counters = Counters(STARTING_BUCKS, BUCK_RATE,
                    STARTING_BUCK_BOOSTER)
```

We also could have written this line of code like so:

```
counters = Counters(15, 120, 1)
```

It would run the exact same way, but we used the variables so that we can easily find and change these numbers later on if we need to.

Count the Game Loops

The next method will keep track of time passing in the game.

We'll have this method run once every game loop. It will add **1** to **loop_count** each time. This way we can keep track of how many times the game loop runs over the course of the game.

▶ **Your Turn**

```
#Counters class, init method
        self.buck_rate = buck_rate
        self.buck_booster = buck_booster
        self.bucks_rect = None
 #To Do: Define a method called update here
 #To Do: Add 1 to the value of loop_count here

class BackgroundTile(sprite.Sprite):
    def __init__(self):
        super().__init__()
```

1. Define a new method called update() that takes only self as an argument.

2. Use the += operator to add 1 to the value of self.loop_count.

It should look like this:

```
def update(self):
    self.loop_count += 1
```

Now every time the game loop runs, the value of `loop_count` will change by one: 0, 1, 2, 3 . . .

Adding and Subtracting Value from a Variable

When you are developing games, you will need to keep track of different types of numbers. For example, you may want to add two points every time a player hits a "goal" with a "ball" sprite. To change the value of a variable every time something happens, we use the following symbols:

`+=` and `-=`

These symbols mean "add a certain amount, then assign the new total to the variable" or "take away a certain amount, then assign the new total to the variable."

For example:

```
if goal:
    score += 2
```

When the the player scores a goal, add **2** to the value of **score**. If the player started with **8** points, the new value of the variable **score** would be **10**.

Earn Points

Next let's define a method that will allow the player to earn pizza bucks based on how many times the game loop runs. Let's set up the game so that the player receives one pizza buck once every **120** times the game loop runs. You'll be able to adjust the rate later on to make the game easier or harder.

We are going to add code that will test for each time **120** game loops have passed (about every 2 seconds) and add **1** to the player's total pizza bucks each time that happens.

>>> **Type This**

```
#Counters class, init method
        self.buck_rate = buck_rate
        self.buck_booster = buck_booster
        self.bucks_rect = None
#Increase the player's pizza bucks based on time passing
    def increment_bucks(self):
#Add a set number of pizza bucks to the player's total once
#every 120 times the game loop runs (approx. every 2 seconds)
        if self.loop_count % self.buck_rate == 0:
            self.pizza_bucks += self.buck_booster
    def update(self):
        self.loop_count += 1
```

Take a Closer Look

```
self.buck_rate = buck_rate
self.buck_booster = buck_booster
self.bucks_rect = None

def increment_bucks(self):
    if self.loop_count % self.buck_rate == 0:
        self.pizza_bucks += self.buck_booster
```

```
if self.loop_count % self.buck_rate == 0:
    self.pizza_bucks += self.buck_booster
```

This code divides the **loop_count** by the **buck_rate** (120), then takes the remainder. If the remainder is 0, then it knows that the current **loop_count** is a multiple of 120.

Every 120th time the game loop runs, we add the value of **buck_booster** (currently 1) to the player's **pizza_bucks** total.

Note: Later on in the game, you will create the ability to add value to the **buck_booster** so that players can lay traps to earn more than one buck at a time.

 **Your Turn**

Now we need to call our new method.

```
#Counters class
        self.pizza_bucks += self.buck_booster

    def update(self):
        self.loop_count += 1
    #To Do: Call the increment_bucks method here

    class BackgroundTile(sprite.Sprite):
        def __init__(self, rect):
            super().__init__()
```

Look at the pattern for calling a method on an object:

self.method_name()

Use the pattern to call the **increment_bucks()** method.

Ideas for Programmers

Modulus

Modulus is an operator like **+**, **-**, or *****. It uses the symbol **%**.

Modulus is related to division. Modulus finds what is left over (the remainder) when dividing numbers. It is a good way to find out if one number goes into another number evenly, without a remainder. In other words, it is a good way to find out if one number is a factor of another number.

For example:

6 ÷ 3 = 2

2 is a whole number without a remainder. The modulus is 0. It would be written like this:

6 % 3 = 0

2 groups

Let's look at another example:

6 ÷ 5 = 1, remainder 1

This is 1 with 1 remaining (left over). The modulus is 1. It would be written like this:

6 % 5 = 1

1 group, with 1 left over

How could we use modulus to test if the value of a variable is even? All even numbers are divisible by two without a remainder.

```
If my_number % 2 == 0:
    print("I am an even number!")
else:
    print("I am an odd number!")
```

We can also use modulus to find multiples of a number.

Let's look at more examples:

Division Problem		Related Modulus Statement
$3 \div 3 = 1$	⬤⬤⬤ ▶	`3 % 3 == 0`
$4 \div 3 = 1$ remainder 1	⬤⬤⬤ ⬤ ▶	`4 % 3 == 1`
$5 \div 3 = 1$ remainder 2	⬤⬤⬤ ⬤⬤ ▶	`5 % 3 == 2`
$6 \div 3 = 2$	⬤⬤⬤ ⬤⬤⬤ ▶	`6 % 3 == 0`
$7 \div 3 = 2$ remainder 1	⬤⬤⬤ ⬤⬤⬤ ⬤ ▶	`7 % 3 == 1`
$8 \div 3 = 2$ remainder 2	⬤⬤⬤ ⬤⬤⬤ ⬤⬤ ▶	`8 % 3 == 2`
$9 \div 3 = 3$	⬤⬤⬤ ⬤⬤⬤ ⬤⬤⬤ ▶	`9 % 3 == 3`

Notice that the numbers equal to 0 in the modulus statements (3, 6, 9) are all multiples of 3. In our example, modulus will be equal to 0 for every multiple of 3.

Imagine we had a program that makes pizzas.

```python
if loop_count % 3 == 0:
    make_pizza()
```

This code would make a new pizza every third time the loop in our pizza-making program runs. Yum!

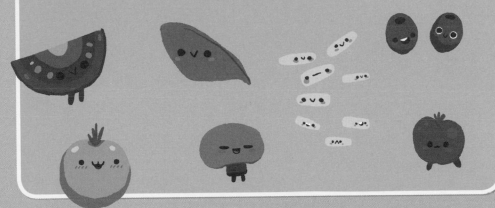

Display Pizza Bucks in the Game Window

The player needs to know how many pizza bucks they have. Even though we are keeping track of the number of bucks players have in the variable `pizza_bucks`, we still need to make that value visible to the player.

The next method that we write will display the value of `pizza_bucks` to the game window.

```
#Counters class
    def increment_bucks(self):
        if self.loop_count % self.buck_rate == 0:
            self.pizza_bucks += self.buck_booster

#Define a new method with two arguments
    def draw_bucks(self, game_window):
#Erase the last number from the game window
        if bool(self.bucks_rect):
            game_window.blit(BACKGROUND, (self.bucks_rect.x,
                            self.bucks_rect.y), self.bucks_rect)
        bucks_surf = self.display_font.render(
                        str(self.pizza_bucks), True, WHITE)
#Create a rect for bucks_surf
        self.bucks_rect = bucks_surf.get_rect()
#Place the counter in the middle of the tile on the
#bottom-right corner
        self.bucks_rect.x = WINDOW_WIDTH – 50
        self.bucks_rect.y = WINDOW_HEIGHT – 50
#Display the new pizza bucks total to the game window
        game_window.blit(bucks_surf, self.bucks_rect)

    def update(self):
        self.loop_count += 1
        self.increment_bucks()
```

Take a Closer Look

```
def draw_bucks(self, game_window):
    if bool(self.bucks_rect):
        game_window.blit(BACKGROUND, (self.bucks_rect.x,
                        self.bucks_rect.y), self.bucks_rect)
    bucks_surf = self.display_font.render(
                    str(self.pizza_bucks),True, WHITE)
    self.bucks_rect = bucks_surf.get_rect()
    self.bucks_rect.x = WINDOW_WIDTH – 50
    self.bucks_rect.y = WINDOW_HEIGHT – 50
    game_window.blit(bucks_surf, self.bucks_rect)
```

```
if bool(self.bucks_rect):
    game_window.blit(BACKGROUND, (self.bucks_rect.x,
                    self.bucks_rect.y), self.bucks_rect)
bucks_surf = self.display_font.render(
                str(self.pizza_bucks), True, WHITE)
self.bucks_rect = bucks_surf.get_rect()
```

If the **bucks_rect** is set to **True** (has any value), then erase the last number from the game window.

Note: Remember, we set it to `None` in the `__init__` method. So this part won't run the first time this method is called because `bucks_rect` won't have a value yet.

 **>>> Type This**

```
#Counters class, draw bucks method
        self.bucks_rect.x = WINDOW_WIDTH – 50
        self.bucks_rect.y = WINDOW_HEIGHT – 50
        game_window.blit(bucks_surf, self.bucks_rect)

    def update(self):
    def update(self, game_window):
        self.loop_count += 1
        self.increment_bucks()
#To Do: Call the draw_bucks method here

class BackgroundTile(sprite.Sprite):
    def __init__(self):
        super().__init__()
```

▶ **Your Turn**

1. Add the argument `game_window` to the `update` method as shown.

2. Call `draw_bucks()` with the argument `game_window`.

Call Update

Now every time `update()` is called, `increment_bucks()` and `draw_bucks()` will also be called. We need to make sure that `update()` is called every time the game loop runs.

Power Up: Remember, when you **call** a method, it means that you are telling the program to run the blocks of code inside that method. Methods won't run unless they are called.

```
#----------------------
#Update displays
for vampire in all_vampires:
    vampire.update(GAME_WINDOW)

#To Do: Call the Counters update method here
display.update()

#Set the frame rate
clock.tick(FRAME_RATE)
```

1. Call the `update()` method on the `counters` instance.

2. Pass in one argument, `GAME_WINDOW`.

   It should look like this:

   ```
   counters.update(GAME_WINDOW)
   ```

Now this method will be called as part of the game loop.

Check Your Work

Run your code to check your work. You should see a number in the lower-right corner that counts up by one. If your program works differently, stop and debug.

TEST
PLAN
BUILD

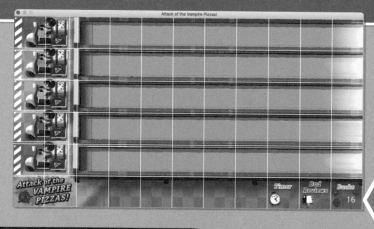

```python
#Set up rates
SPAWN_RATE = 360
FRAME_RATE = 60

#Set up counters
STARTING_BUCKS = 15
BUCK_RATE = 120
STARTING_BUCK_BOOSTER = 1

#Define speeds
REG_SPEED = 2
SLOW_SPEED = 1

#-------------------------------------------------
```

```python
#VampireSprite class

    #Set up enemy movement
    def update(self, game_window):
        game_window.blit(BACKGROUND,
                         (self.rect.x, self.rect.y), self.rect)
        self.rect.x -= self.speed
        game_window.blit(self.image, (self.rect.x, self.rect.y))

#Create an object for tracking the game state
class Counters(object):

    #Set up instances of counters
    def __init__(self, pizza_bucks, buck_rate, buck_booster):
        self.loop_count = 0
        self.display_font = font.Font('pizza_font.ttf', 25)
        self.pizza_bucks = pizza_bucks
        self.buck_rate = buck_rate
        self.buck_booster = buck_booster
        self.bucks_rect = None

    #Set the rate that the player earns pizza bucks
    def increment_bucks(self):
        if self.loop_count % self.buck_rate == 0:
            self.pizza_bucks += self.buck_booster
```

```python
    #Display pizza bucks total on the screen
    def draw_bucks(self, game_window):
        if bool(self.bucks_rect):
            game_window.blit(BACKGROUND, (self.bucks_rect.x,
                            self.bucks_rect.y), self.bucks_rect)
        bucks_surf = self.display_font.render(
                    str(self.pizza_bucks), True, WHITE)
        self.bucks_rect = bucks_surf.get_rect()
        self.bucks_rect.x = WINDOW_WIDTH - 50
        self.bucks_rect.y = WINDOW_HEIGHT - 50
        game_window.blit(bucks_surf, self.bucks_rect)

    #Increment the loop counter and call the other Counters methods
    def update(self, game_window):
        self.loop_count += 1
        self.increment_bucks()
        self.draw_bucks(game_window)

#Create a background tile object
class BackgroundTile(sprite.Sprite):

    #Set up instances of background tiles
    def __init__(self, rect):
        super().__init__()
        self.effect = False
        self.rect = rect

#------------------------------------------------
#Create class instances and groups

#Create a group for all VampireSprite instances
all_vampires = sprite.Group()

#Create an instance of Counters
counters = Counters(STARTING_BUCKS, BUCK_RATE,
                    STARTING_BUCK_BOOSTER)

#------------------------------------------------
#Initialize and draw the background grid

#Create an empty list to hold tile grid
tile_grid = []
#Define color of the grid outline
tile_color = WHITE
```

```
#----------------------
#Update displays

#Update enemies
for vampire in all_vampires:
    vampire.update(GAME_WINDOW)

#Update counters
counters.update(GAME_WINDOW)

#Update all the images on the screen
display.update()

#Set the frame rate
clock.tick(FRAME_RATE)

#------------------------------------------------
#Close main game loop
```

Level Up!

0 1 2 3 4 5 6 7 8 9 10 11 12 13 ★

You added a points system to your game! This system keeps track of time passing, adds points over time, and displays the player's current total points. You learned:

1. To add value to a variable total
2. To use modulus % to control how frequently something happens in the game

You practiced:

1. Creating an object
2. Defining new methods and attributes
3. Passing in arguments when calling a method or creating an attribute

Stupendous! Splendid! Superb!

Chapter 11

Applying Traps

We've set up a system for earning pizza bucks, and we've set up a collision-detection system that slows down a vampire pizza when it touches a tile that was clicked by the player.

> **Now that these systems are set up, we want to do two things:**
>
> 1. We want the systems to work together so the player can purchase a trap by spending pizza bucks.
>
> 2. We want to create the ability to lay different types of traps, not just slow traps.

Hey, this is a tutorial. Why do I have to keep changing the code that I just wrote?

That is a great question! I could show you the code for the final game line by line and have you type it in.

But this book is all about learning how to code, and coding can be messy! Program developers use **computational thinking** skills to create solutions to problems and to express themselves creatively. This tutorial is following the natural process of game development.

First, we imagine a game: *Attack of the Vampire Pizzas!* We know how we want the game to work. We come up with the concept and the rules. Then we have to use a skill called **decomposition** to break down that game into pieces that we can build. For example, the clickable grid, collision detection, and the pizza bucks points system are all parts of the game that we had to build. We have to set up the parts, then revise them to work together.

Another skill that we have to use is **abstraction**. When we created collision detection, the slow trap was built right into it. This is like creating a tool that we can only use in one way. But if we create a class of traps, it allows us to create and use as many types of traps as we want. **When we make a new class, we are making an object that we can reuse. When we set up a new method, we are creating an action that we can reuse. Putting code into these reusable "containers" is called abstraction.** This is like creating a tool that can be used in different ways at different times. Many times when we refactor, it is because it was easier to develop something right into the game loop, but we can make the game more flexible if we go back and see where it's possible to turn something into a reusable tool.

We need a class of objects that includes all the types of effects that we might apply to tiles in our background grid.

Trap Types

In our game, every pizza shop owner knows two things: how to make pizza, and how to destroy vampire pizza.

First, you'll need garlic—lots of garlic—to slow down the vampire pizzas in their tracks. They call this the Van Helstink maneuver. It will cut their speed in half.

Second, you'll need wooden pizza cutters, which are like wooden stakes but are specifically designed for pizza-shaped vampires. They do damage that will destroy the pizzas over time.

Third, you'll need pepperoni to earn pizza bucks faster, so you can buy more traps!

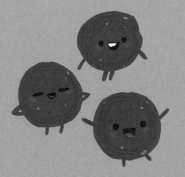

Before we set up the new class, let's load the images for each trap into our program. When the player selects a trap and clicks on a tile, it will place an image so that the player knows what has been put there.

We'll start with a garlic trap. This will cause the vampire pizzas to slow down. We'll use the same pattern that we used to add the other images. If you look back at your code, you can see that we used three lines of code for each image.

We loaded the image, converted it to a surface, and then scaled it to the size that we want.

>>> **Type This**

```
#Set up the enemy image
pizza_img = image.load('vampire.png')
pizza_surf = Surface.convert_alpha(pizza_img)
VAMPIRE_PIZZA = transform.scale(pizza_surf, (WIDTH, HEIGHT))

#Set up trap images
garlic_img = image.load('garlic.png')
garlic_surf = Surface.convert_alpha(garlic_img)
GARLIC = transform.scale(garlic_surf, (WIDTH, HEIGHT))

#----------------------------------------------
#Set up class objects
class VampireSprite(sprite.Sprite):
    def __init__(self):
        super().__init__()
```

```
#Set up trap images
garlic_img = image.load('garlic.png')
garlic_surf = Surface.convert_alpha(garlic_img)
GARLIC = transform.scale(garlic_surf, (WIDTH, HEIGHT))

#To Do: Load pizza cutter image
#To Do: Convert pizza cutter to a surface
#To Do: Set the size of the pizza cutter

#To Do: Use 3 lines of code to import and set up the
#pepperoni image


#---------------------------------------------
#Set up classes
class VampireSprite(sprite.Sprite):
    def __init__(self):
        super().__init__()
```

You can import the other two images.

1. Import `'pizzacutter.png'`. Store it in a variable called `cutter_img`.

2. Convert `cutter_img` and store it in a new variable called `cutter_surf`.

3. Scale `cutter_surf` using the same width and height as the garlic. Store it in a variable called `CUTTER`.

4. Import `'pepperoni.png'`. Use the same pattern to convert the image to a surface and scale it to the same width and height as the other two. Store your scaled image in a variable called `PEPPERONI`. Then give it the same alpha as the other two.

You can check your work at the end of the chapter.

Trap Class

Now we can set up the trap object. This will let us create any number of traps we want.

>>> **Type This**

```python
#Counters class
    def update(self, game_window):
        self.loop_count += 1
        self.increment_bucks()
        self.draw_bucks(game_window)

#Set up the different kinds of traps
class Trap(object):
    def __init__(self, trap_kind, cost, trap_img):
        self.trap_kind = trap_kind
        self.cost = cost
        self.trap_img = trap_img

class BackgroundTile(sprite.Sprite):
    def __init__(self, rect):
        super().__init__()
```

Now that we've created the class, let's create an instance of each type of trap. The instances will take values to pass to the `trap_kind`, `cost`, and `trap_img` arguments.

>>> **Type This**

```python
#------------------------------------------
#Create class instances and sprite groups
all_vampires = sprite.Group()
counters = Counters(STARTING_BUCKS, BUCK_RATE,
                    STARTING_BUCK_BOOSTER)
SLOW = Trap('SLOW', 5, GARLIC)
DAMAGE = Trap('DAMAGE', 3, CUTTER)
#To Do: Add EARN trap here

#------------------------------------------
#Initialize and draw the background grid
tile_grid = []
tile_color = WHITE
for row in range(6):
```

 **Your Turn**

Create the last trap on your own.

1. Create a trap called `EARN`.

2. The **trap_type** is `'EARN'`. It costs `7` pizza bucks and uses the `PEPPERONI` image.

When we create a trap, we are passing in three pieces of information. The first argument is the trap type. The next is the number of pizza bucks it costs to buy the trap. The last argument is the image used for each trap.

Trap Applicator

In the last section, you created a trap object. But now we need a separate tool to select traps and apply them to tiles.
We'll call this object `TrapApplicator`.

 **Your Turn**

```
#Trap class
        self.trap_kind = trap_kind
        self.cost = cost
        self.trap_img = trap_img

#To Do: Create a class called TrapApplicator here
#To Do: Define an __init__ method here
#To Do: Add an attribute called selected here

#To Do: Define the select_trap method here
#To Do: Test if cost is less than or equal to pizza bucks
#To Do: If it is, change the value of the self.selected

class BackgroundTile(sprite.Sprite):
    def __init__(self, rect):
        super().__init__()
```

1. Create a class called `TrapApplicator` with `object` as its base class.

2. Define an `__init__` method that takes the argument `self`.

3. Create an attribute called `selected` and set the value to `None`.

4. Define another method called `select_trap` with two arguments: `self` and `trap`.

5. Test if `trap.cost` is less than or equal to `counters.pizza_bucks`.

6. If the test is **True**, change the value of the `selected` attribute to `trap`. This way, the player only gets to set the trap if they have enough pizza bucks to purchase it.

You can check your work at the end of the chapter.

Finally, we'll set up a method that will select the background tile where we want to lay the trap:

>>> **Type This**

```
#TrapApplicator class
    def select_trap(self, trap):
        if trap.cost <= counters.pizza_bucks:
            self.selected = trap

    def select_tile(self, tile, counters):
        self.selected = tile.set_trap(self.selected, counters)

class BackgroundTile(sprite.Sprite):
    def __init__(self, rect):
        super().__init__()
```

Take a Closer Look

```
#TrapApplicator class
    def select_trap(self, trap):
        if trap.cost <= counters.pizza_bucks:
            self.selected = trap

    def select_tile(self, tile, counters):
        self.selected = tile.set_trap(self.selected, counters)

class BackgroundTile(sprite.Sprite):
    def __init__(self, rect):
        super().__init__()
```

```
def select_tile(self, tile, counters):
    self.selected = tile.set_trap(self.selected, counters)
```

The `select_tile()` method places the selected trap on the selected tile.

Note: We'll make the `set_trap()` method in the next chapter, so don't worry if you don't understand it yet.

So to recap, the **TrapApplicator** is just an object that keeps track of which trap the player wants to use and the tile on which the player wants to add the trap. Before we move on, let's create an instance of the **TrapApplicator** object.

▶ Your Turn

```
SLOW = Trap('SLOW', 5, GARLIC)
DAMAGE = Trap('DAMAGE', 3, CUTTER)
EARN = Trap('EARN', 7, PEPPERONI)

#To Do: Create TrapApplicator instance here

#------------------------------------------------
#Initialize and draw background grid
tile_grid = []
tile_color = WHITE
for row in range(6):
```

Look at the pattern for creating and naming a class instance:

variable_name = ClassName()

Create an instance of `TrapApplicator`, and name it `trap_applicator`.

Connect TrapApplicator to Click Event

The **TrapApplicator** should be able to detect whether a tile was clicked. So we need to incorporate it into the **MOUSEBUTTONDOWN** event in the game loop. To do this, we'll change the line at the end of the event to use the **TrapApplicator** tool.

The new line tells our program that the tile the player clicked on is where they want to lay a trap.

>>> **Type This**

```
        if event.type == QUIT:
            game_running = False

#Set up background tiles to respond to mouse click
        elif event.type == MOUSEBUTTONDOWN:
            coordinates = mouse.get_pos()
            x = coordinates[0]
            y = coordinates[1]
            tile_y = y // 100
            tile_x = x // 100
            tile_grid[tile_y][tile_x].effect = True
            trap_applicator.select_tile(
                    tile_grid[tile_y][tile_x], counters)


    #-------------------------------------------------
    #Spawn vampire pizza sprites
        if randint(1, SPAWN_RATE) == 1:
            VampireSprite()
```

Check Your Work

Usually, you run your code to see if it works. But this time, we know it doesn't work, because you haven't written one of the methods that we used in the code in this chapter. In the next section, we will create the **set_trap** method and get the code running. For now, you can compare your code to mine.

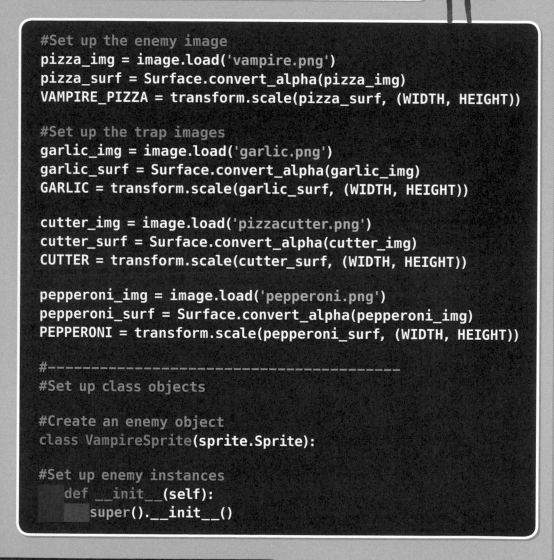

```python
#Set up the enemy image
pizza_img = image.load('vampire.png')
pizza_surf = Surface.convert_alpha(pizza_img)
VAMPIRE_PIZZA = transform.scale(pizza_surf, (WIDTH, HEIGHT))

#Set up the trap images
garlic_img = image.load('garlic.png')
garlic_surf = Surface.convert_alpha(garlic_img)
GARLIC = transform.scale(garlic_surf, (WIDTH, HEIGHT))

cutter_img = image.load('pizzacutter.png')
cutter_surf = Surface.convert_alpha(cutter_img)
CUTTER = transform.scale(cutter_surf, (WIDTH, HEIGHT))

pepperoni_img = image.load('pepperoni.png')
pepperoni_surf = Surface.convert_alpha(pepperoni_img)
PEPPERONI = transform.scale(pepperoni_surf, (WIDTH, HEIGHT))

#------------------------------------------------
#Set up class objects

#Create an enemy object
class VampireSprite(sprite.Sprite):

#Set up enemy instances
    def __init__(self):
        super().__init__()
```

```python
#Counters class
    def update(self, game_window):
        self.loop_count += 1
        self.increment_bucks()
        self.draw_bucks(game_window)

#Create a trap object
class Trap(object):

#Set up instances of each kind of trap
    def __init__(self, trap_kind, cost, trap_img):
        self.trap_kind = trap_kind
        self.cost = cost
        self.trap_img = trap_img

#Create an object that activates traps
class TrapApplicator(object):

    #Set up TrapApplicator instances
    def __init__(self):
        self.selected = None

    #Activate a trap button
    def select_trap(self, trap):
        if trap.cost <= counters.pizza_bucks:
            self.selected = trap

    #Lay a trap on a specific tile
    def select_tile(self, tile, counters):
        self.selected = tile.set_trap(self.selected, counters)

#Create a background tile object
class BackgroundTile(sprite.Sprite):

#Set up instances of background tiles
    def __init__(self, rect):
        super().__init__()
```

```
#----------------------------------------------------------
#Create class instances and groups

#Create a group for all VampireSprite instances
all_vampires = sprite.Group()

#Create an instance of Counters
counters = Counters(STARTING_BUCKS, BUCK_RATE,
                    STARTING_BUCK_BOOSTER)

#Create instances of each kind of trap
SLOW = Trap('SLOW', 5, GARLIC)
DAMAGE = Trap('DAMAGE', 3, CUTTER)
EARN = Trap('EARN', 7, PEPPERONI)

#Create an instance of the TrapApplicator
trap_applicator = TrapApplicator()


#----------------------------------------------------------
#Initialize and draw the background grid

#Create an empty list to hold tile grid
tile_grid = []

#Define the color of the grid outline
tile_color = WHITE

#Populate the background grid
for row in range(6):
```

Level Up!

0 1 2 3 4 5 6 7 8 9 10 **11** 12 13 ★

Wonderful! You used your knowledge of classes, methods, and attributes to complete the first steps to adding traps to your game!

Chapter 12

Connecting Traps to the Grid

In this chapter we will take the traps we made in Chapter 11 and add two more things:

1. The ability to allow the player to add traps to the background tiles.

2. The ability to apply the traps to the vampire pizzas that collide with those tiles.

Tile Subclasses

We've got our three types of traps: **slow**, **damage**, and **earn.** But now we need to prepare someplace for them to go in our game. Remember, our entire background is a grid of tiles. We're going to need three types of background tiles to select and lay the traps.

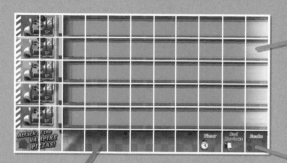

Play Tile: This is the main play area. A player can lay traps on these tiles.

Inactive Tile: These tiles will be used to display information, such as the game clock and pizza bucks. Players can't lay traps here.

Button Tile: We'll turn these three tiles into buttons that the player can use to select each trap type.

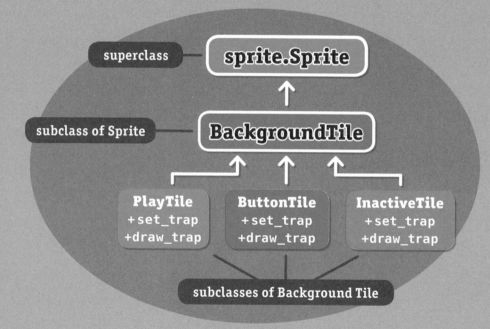

superclass — **sprite.Sprite**

subclass of Sprite — **BackgroundTile**

PlayTile
+set_trap
+draw_trap

ButtonTile
+set_trap
+draw_trap

InactiveTile
+set_trap
+draw_trap

subclasses of Background Tile

We'll start by replacing `effect` with a new attribute `trap`. Trap will either have a value of `None` or of one of the trap types: `SLOW`, `DAMAGE`, or `EARN`.

Then we will create a subclass for each of the three kinds of tiles.

We'll also add a `set_trap()` and a `draw_trap()` method for each of the subclasses.

```python
#Base class for all tiles
class BackgroundTile(sprite.Sprite):
    def __init__(self, rect):
        super().__init__()
        self.effect = False
        self.trap = None
        self.rect = rect
#A subclass of BackgroundTile where the player can set traps
class PlayTile(BackgroundTile):
#Set the trap on the selected play tile
    def set_trap(self, trap, counters):
        if bool(trap) and not bool(self.trap):
            counters.pizza_bucks -= trap.cost
            self.trap = trap
            if trap == EARN:
                counters.buck_booster += 1
        return None
#Draw the trap image to the selected play tile
    def draw_trap(self, game_window, trap_applicator):
        if bool(self.trap):
            game_window.blit(self.trap.trap_img,
                             (self.rect.x, self.rect.y))


#------------------------------------------------
#Create class instances
all_vampires = sprite.Group()
counters = Counters(STARTING_BUCKS, BUCK_RATE,
                    STARTING_BUCK_BOOSTER)
SLOW = Trap('SLOW', 5, GARLIC)
```

We'll use the same pattern from the PlayTile subclass to make
the ButtonTile and InactiveTile subclasses.

All of the tile subclasses will have the same two methods:
set_trap and draw_trap. But these methods will do different
things for each type of tile.

```
#PlayTile class
    def draw_trap(self, game_window, trap_applicator):
        if bool(self.trap):
            game_window.blit(self.trap.trap img,
                             (self.rect.x, self.rect.y))
```

```
#To Do: Create the ButtonTile class here
#To Do: Define the set_trap method here
#To Do: Test if the player has enough pizza bucks here
#To Do: If player has enough pizza bucks, return self.trap
#To Do: Else
#To Do: Return trap
#To Do: Define the draw_trap method here
#To Do: Test if selected is True and if selected is equal
#to self.trap
#To Do: If the test is True, draw a rectangle on the
#selected button tile
#To Do: Create the InactiveTile class here
#To Do: Define the set_trap method here
#To Do: Return trap
#To Do: Define the draw_trap method here
#To Do: Pass
```

```
#------------------------------------------------
#Create class instances and groups
all_vampires = sprite.Group()
counters = Counters(STARTING_BUCKS, BUCK_RATE,
                    STARTING_BUCK_BOOSTER)
SLOW = Trap('SLOW', 5, GARLIC)
```

Let's start with `ButtonTile`. Button tiles are tiles that the player can click on to select which trap they would like to set.

1. Create a class called `ButtonTile` with `BackgroundTile` as the base class.

2. Define a method called `set_trap` that takes the arguments `self`, `trap`, and `counters`.

3. Test if `counters.pizza_bucks` is greater than or equal to `self.trap.cost`.

4. If the test is True, `return` `self.trap`. Otherwise, `return` `None`.

5. Define a method called `draw_trap` that takes the arguments `self`, `game_window`, and `trap_applicator`.

6. Test if `trap_applicator.selected` is True.

7. If it is True, then test if `trap_applicator.selected` is equal to `self.trap`.

8. If that test is True, draw a border around the button:

```
        draw.rect(game_window, (238, 190, 47),
                    (self.rect.x, self.rect.y, WIDTH, HEIGHT), 5)
```

Check Your Work Before your create the next class, pause to check your work. The **ButtonTile** class should look like this:

```
#Playtile class
    def draw_trap(self, game_window, trap_applicator):
        if bool(self.trap):
            game_window.blit(self.trap.trap img,
                            (self.rect.x, self.rect.y))

class ButtonTile(BackgroundTile):
    def set_trap(self, trap, counters):
        if counters.pizza_bucks >= self.trap.cost:
            return self.trap
        else:
            return None

    def draw_trap(self, game_window, trap_applicator):
        if bool(trap_applicator.selected):
            if trap_applicator.selected == self.trap:
                draw.rect(game_window, (238, 190, 47),
                            (self.rect.x, self.rect.y, WIDTH, HEIGHT), 5)

#-------------------------------------------------
#Create class instances and groups
all_vampires = sprite.Group()
counters = Counters(STARTING_BUCKS, BUCK_RATE,
                    STARTING_BUCK_BOOSTER)
SLOW = Trap('SLOW', 5, GARLIC)
```

We have one final tile type to add: the `InactiveTile`. Inactive tiles are any tiles that aren't part of the active game area and cannot have traps on them.

1. Create a class called `InactiveTile` with `BackgroundTile` as the base class.

2. Define a method called `set_trap` that takes the arguments `self`, `trap`, and `counters`.

3. Have the method `return` `None`.

4. Define a method called `draw_trap` that takes the arguments `self`, `game_window`, and `trap_applicator`.

5. Type the word `pass` inside the method. This is a keyword that tells the method to do nothing.

You can check your work at the end of the chapter.

> Why do we need the `InactiveTile` class if it doesn't do anything? If the player clicks on an inactive tile, we don't want anything to happen, but we also don't want it to cause an error. By creating this class, we are telling the program that nothing is supposed to happen.

Connect Tile Types to Background Grid

We made the tile subclasses. Now we have to incorporate them into the background grid. We have to label which parts of the grid are which type of tile and create instances at those locations.

```
#------------------------------------------------
#Initialize and draw the background grid
tile_grid = []
tile_color = WHITE
for row in range(6):
    row_of_tiles = []
    tile_grid.append(row_of_tiles)
    for column in range(11):
        tile_rect = Rect(WIDTH * column, HEIGHT * row,
                         WIDTH, HEIGHT)
        new_tile = BackgroundTile(tile_rect)
        if column <= 1:
            new_tile = InactiveTile(tile_rect)
        else:
            if row == 5:
                if 2 <= column <= 4:
                    new_tile = ButtonTile(tile_rect)
                    new_tile.trap = [SLOW, DAMAGE, EARN][column - 2]
                else:
                    new_tile = InactiveTile(tile_rect)
            else:
                new_tile = PlayTile(tile_rect)
        row_of_tiles.append(new_tile)
        if row == 5 and 2 <= column <= 4:
            BACKGROUND.blit(new_tile.trap.trap_img,
                            (new_tile.rect.x, new_tile.rect.y))
        draw.rect(BACKGROUND, tile_color, (WIDTH * column,
                  HEIGHT * row, WIDTH, HEIGHT), 1)
        if column != 0 and row != 5:
            if column != 1:
                draw.rect(BACKGROUND, tile_color, (WIDTH * column,
                          HEIGHT * row, WIDTH, HEIGHT), 1)

GAME_WINDOW.blit(BACKGROUND, (0,0))

#------------------------------------------------
#Game loop
game_running = True
while game_running:
```

Take a Closer Look

Let's look at the new code in detail.

```
if column <= 1:
    new_tile = InactiveTile(tile_rect)
```

If the tiles are in the first two columns, which have the pizza boxes in them, they will be labeled InactiveTile.

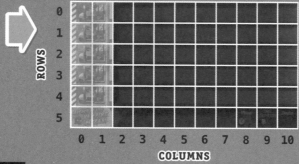

```
else:
    if row == 5:
        if 2 <= column <= 4:
            new_tile = ButtonTile(tile_rect)
            new_tile.trap = [SLOW, DAMAGE, EARN][column - 2]
```

If we are in any other column, the program will do some other tests. First, it will test if we are in the bottom row. If we are in the bottom row *and* we are in columns 2, 3, or 4, then it will label the tiles ButtonTile. The last line tells the program what each ButtonTile is in order (SLOW , DAMAGE , and EARN).

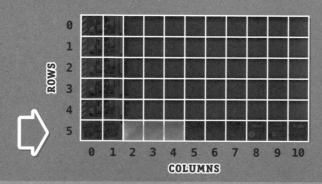

```
            else:
                new_tile = InactiveTile(tile_rect)
```

If we are in the bottom row but NOT in columns 2, 3, or 4, then it
will label the rest of the tiles `InactiveTile`. That's where our
score and timer are displayed.

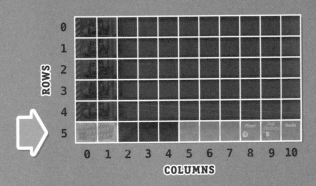

```
            else:
                new_tile = PlayTile(tile_rect)
```

If we're not in the first two columns or the bottom row, the
program will label all the other tiles `PlayTile`.

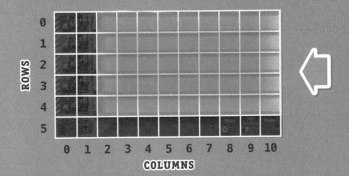

```
if row == 5 and 2 <= column <= 4:
    BACKGROUND.blit(new_tile.trap.trap_img,
                    (new_tile.rect.x, new_tile.rect.y))
```

This tests if the tile is one of the three buttons and displays
the correct image on each button.

```
    if column != 0 and row != 5:
        if column != 1:
            draw.rect(BACKGROUND, tile_color, (WIDTH * column,
                      HEIGHT * row, WIDTH, HEIGHT), 1)
```

This tests if we're anywhere OTHER than a button and
displays the background image.

Draw the Traps onto the Grid

Just like the vampire pizza sprites, we need to update the trap
images by erasing and redrawing them each time the game loop runs.
We'll use nested loops to check and update each tile on the grid.
First we'll erase the trap from the last game loop.

>>> **Type This**

```
#Spawn vampire pizza sprites
    if randint(1, SPAWN_RATE) == 1:
        VampireSprite()

    for tile_row in tile_grid:
        for tile in tile_row:
            if bool(tile.trap):
                GAME_WINDOW.blit(BACKGROUND, (tile.rect.x,
                                 tile.rect.y), tile.rect)

#------------------------------------------------
#Set up detection for collision with background tiles
    for vampire in all_vampires:
        tile_row = tile_grid[vampire.rect.y // 100]
        vamp_left_side = vampire.rect.x // 100
```

Now let's draw the updated traps.

```
#------------------------------------------------
#Update displays
    for vampire in all_vampires:
#Add a new argument to the update method for VampireSprite
-       vampire.update(GAME_WINDOW)
+       vampire.update(GAME_WINDOW, counters)

+       for tile_row in tile_grid:
            for tile in tile_row:
                tile.draw_trap(GAME_WINDOW, trap_applicator)

    counters.update(GAME_WINDOW)
    display.update()

#Set the frame rate
    clock.tick(FRAME_RATE)
```

Now the program will redraw the trap every time the game loops.

Attack the Vampires

By creating the tile subclasses, we made it possible to attach traps to certain tiles. Now we need the traps to attack the vampires when the vampires hit those tiles. To do this, we'll create a new method in the `VampireSprite` class.

The only two types of traps that affect vampire pizzas are `SLOW` and `DAMAGE`. The `EARN` trap adds pizza bucks and won't interact with the vampire pizzas.

```
#VampireSprite class, init method
    self.image = VAMPIRE_PIZZA.copy()
    y = 50 + self.lane * 100
    self.rect = self.image.get_rect(center = (1100, y))

#VampireSprite class
#Add a counters argument to the update method so that we can
#change the health and speed of vampire pizzas
-   def update(self, game_window):
+   def update(self, game_window, counters):
        game_window.blit(BACKGROUND,
                                (self.rect.x, self.rect.y), self.rect)
        self.rect.x -= self.speed
        game_window.blit(self.image, (self.rect.x, self.rect.y))

+   def attack(self, tile):
        if tile.trap == SLOW:
            self.speed = SLOW_SPEED
!   #To Do: Test for the DAMAGE trap here
    #To Do: Apply the DAMAGE effect to the vampire pizza here

class Counters(object):
    def __init__(self, pizza_bucks, buck_rate, buck_booster):
        self.loop_count = 0
```

Take a Closer Look

```
#VampireSprite class
    def update(self, game_window, counters):
        game_window.blit(BACKGROUND,
                                (self.rect.x, self.rect.y), self.rect)
        self.rect.x -= self.speed
        game_window.blit(self.image, (self.rect.x, self.rect.y))

    def attack(self, tile):
        if tile.trap == SLOW:
            self.speed = SLOW_SPEED
```

```
if tile.trap == SLOW :
    self.speed = SLOW_SPEED
```

This tests if the vampire pizza touched a tile with a slow trap on it. If so, it changes the vampire pizza's speed from REG_SPEED to SLOW_SPEED.

Your Turn

Next test if the selected trap is `DAMAGE` and apply the effect. Use the lines of code you just wrote to test for the `SLOW` trap as a guide.

1. Test if the selected `trap` is `DAMAGE`.

2. If so, subtract `1` from the value of `self.health` each time the game loop runs.

You can check your work at the end of the chapter.

> **BUT WAIT!** We just created a damage effect that subtracts health points from the vampire pizzas. But we haven't set up the vampire pizzas to *have* any health points. Let's go back and do that.

We're going into the VampireSprite `__init__` method in order to add a starting health value.

Your Turn

```
#VampireSprite class, init method
        all_vampires.add(self)
        self.image = VAMPIRE_PIZZA.copy()
        y = 50 + self.lane * 100
        self.rect = self.image.get_rect(center = (1100, y))
#To Do: Create an attribute called health here

    def update(self, game_window, counters):
        game_window.blit(BACKGROUND,
                        (self.rect.x, self.rect.y), self.rect)
        self.rect.x -= self.speed
```

1. Create a new attribute called `health`.

2. Set the starting value to `100`.

Next we need to destroy the vampire pizza when its health reaches zero or when it reaches the pizza boxes at the end of the row.

We'll test if the vampire pizza health points are zero or if it has reached the pizza boxes. If so, we'll destroy the vampire pizza. If they are not at zero, we'll display the image as we normally would.

>>> Type This

```
#VampireSprite class
    def update(self, game_window, counters):
        game_window.blit(BACKGROUND,
                         (self.rect.x, self.rect.y), self.rect)
        self.rect.x -= self.speed
        game_window.blit(self.image, (self.rect.x, self.rect.y))
        if self.health <= 0 or self.rect.x <= 100:
            self.kill()
        else:
            game_window.blit(self.image, (self.rect.x, self.rect.y))

    def attack(self, tile):
        if tile.trap == SLOW:
            self.speed = SLOW_SPEED
```

Connect Attack Method with Collision Detection

Right now in our game loop, every time a VampireSprite collides with a trap, we've told it to slow down. But we have three different types of traps, so instead of slowing down, we need to tell it to apply the effect of each trap. We can also remove the kill method from this code block, because we just added it into the VampireSprite update method.

```
            if 0 <= vamp_right_side <= 10:
                right_tile = tile_row[vamp_right_side]
            else:
                right_tile = None
        if bool(left_tile) and left_tile.effect:
            vampire.speed = SLOW_SPEED
        if bool(left_tile):
            vampire.attack(left_tile)
        if bool(right_tile) and right_tile.effect:
        if bool(right_tile):
            if right_tile != left_tile:
                vampire.speed = SLOW_SPEED
                vampire.attack(right_tile)
        if vampire.rect.x <= 0:
            vampire.kill()


#----------------------------------------------
#Update displays
    for vampire in all_vampires:
        vampire.update(GAME_WINDOW, counters)
```

Check Your Work

Make sure to run your code. Select and lay
some traps to see what happens. Are the
vampire pizzas responding how they should?
If not, stop and debug your code.

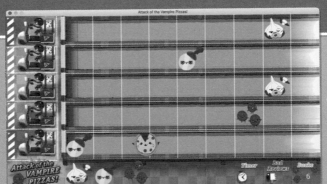

```python
#Create an enemy object
class VampireSprite(sprite.Sprite):

    #Set up enemy instances
    def __init__(self):
        super().__init__()
        self.speed = REG_SPEED
        self.lane = randint(0, 4)
        all_vampires.add(self)
        self.image = VAMPIRE_PIZZA.copy()
        y = 50 + self.lane * 100
        self.rect = self.image.get_rect(center = (1100, y))
        self.health = 100

    #Set up enemy movement
    def update(self, game_window, counters):
        game_window.blit(BACKGROUND,
                        (self.rect.x, self.rect.y), self.rect)
        self.rect.x -= self.speed
        if self.health <= 0 or self.rect.x <= 100:
            self.kill()
        else:
            game_window.blit(self.image, (self.rect.x, self.rect.y))

    #Apply trap effects to enemies
    def attack(self, tile):
        if tile.trap == SLOW:
            self.speed = SLOW_SPEED
        if tile.trap == DAMAGE:
            self.health -= 1

#Create an object for tracking the game state
class Counters(object):
    #Set up instances of counters
    def __init__(self, pizza_bucks, buck_rate, buck_booster):


#Create a background tile object
class BackgroundTile(sprite.Sprite):

    #Set up instances of background tiles
    def __init__(self, rect):
        super().__init__()
        self.trap = None
        self.rect = rect
```

```python
#Create a subclass for tiles in the play area
class PlayTile(BackgroundTile):

    #Lay traps on tiles in the play area
    def set_trap(self, trap, counters):
        if bool(trap) and not bool(self.trap):
            counters.pizza_bucks -= trap.cost
            self.trap = trap
            if trap == EARN:
                counters.buck_booster += 1
        return None

    #Display trap images on tiles in the play area
    def draw_trap(self, game_window, trap_applicator):
        if bool(self.trap):
            game_window.blit(self.trap.trap_img, (self.rect.x,
                             self.rect.y))

#Create a subclass for tiles that are trap buttons
class ButtonTile(BackgroundTile):

    #Click on a trap button to select the trap
    def set_trap(self, trap, counters):
        if counters.pizza_bucks >= self.trap.cost:
            return self.trap
        else:
            return None

    #Highlight the trap button that was clicked
    def draw_trap(self, game_window, trap_applicator):
        if bool(trap_applicator.selected):
            if trap_applicator.selected == self.trap:
                draw.rect(game_window, (238, 190, 47),
                          (self.rect.x, self.rect.y, WIDTH, HEIGHT), 5)

#Create a subclass for tiles that are not interactive
class InactiveTile(BackgroundTile):

    #Do nothing if clicked
    def set_trap(self, trap, counters):
        return None

    #Do not display anything
    def draw_trap(self, game_window, trap_applicator):
        pass

#-------------------------------------------------
```

```
#-----------------------------------------------
#Initialize and draw the background grid

#Create an empty list to hold tile grid
tile_grid = []
#Define the color of the grid outline
tile_color = WHITE

#Populate the background grid
for row in range(6):
    row_of_tiles = []
    tile_grid.append(row_of_tiles)
    for column in range(11):
        tile_rect = Rect(WIDTH * column, HEIGHT * row,
                         WIDTH, HEIGHT)
        if column <= 1:
            new_tile = InactiveTile(tile_rect)
        else:
            if row == 5:
                if 2 <= column <= 4:
                    new_tile = ButtonTile(tile_rect)
                    new_tile.trap = [SLOW, DAMAGE, EARN][column - 2]
                else:
                    new_tile = InactiveTile(tile_rect)
            else:
                new_tile = PlayTile(tile_rect)
        row_of_tiles.append(new_tile)
        if row == 5 and 2 <= column <= 4:
            BACKGROUND.blit(new_tile.trap.trap_img,
                            (new_tile.rect.x, new_tile.rect.y))
        if column != 0 and row != 5:
            if column != 1:
                draw.rect(BACKGROUND, tile_color, (WIDTH * column,
                          HEIGHT * row, WIDTH, HEIGHT), 1)
#Display the background image to the screen
GAME_WINDOW.blit(BACKGROUND, (0,0))

#-----------------------------------------------
#Game loop

#Define the conditions for running the loop
game_running = True

#Start game loop
while game_running:
```

```python
#----------------------
#Spawn sprites

#Spawn vampire pizza sprites
if randint(1, SPAWN_RATE) == 1:
    VampireSprite()


#----------------------
#Set up collision detection

#Draw the background grid
for tile_row in tile_grid:
    for tile in tile_row:
        if bool(tile.trap):
            GAME_WINDOW.blit(BACKGROUND, (tile.rect.x,
                             tile.rect.y), tile.rect)

#Set up detection for collision with background tiles
for vampire in all_vampires:
    tile_row = tile_grid[vampire.rect.y // 100]
    vamp_left_side = vampire.rect.x // 100
    vamp_right_side = (vampire.rect.x +
                       vampire.rect.width) // 100

    if 0 <= vamp_left_side <= 10:
        left_tile = tile_row[vamp_left_side]
    else:
        left_tile = None
    if 0 <= vamp_right_side <= 10:
        right_tile = tile_row[vamp_right_side]
    else:
        right_tile = None
    if bool(left_tile):
        vampire.attack(left_tile)
    if bool(right_tile):
        if right_tile != left_tile:
            vampire.attack(right_tile)


#----------------------
#Update displays

#Update enemies
for vampire in all_vampires:
    vampire.update(GAME_WINDOW, counters)
```

```
#Update traps that have been set
for tile_row in tile_grid:
    for tile in tile_row:
        tile.draw_trap(GAME_WINDOW, trap_applicator)

#Update counters
counters.update(GAME_WINDOW)

#Update all images on the screen
display.update()

#Set the frame rate
clock.tick(FRAME_RATE)

#--------------------------------------------------
#Close main game loop

#Clean up the game
pygame.quit()
```

Level Up!

0   1   2   3   4   5   6   7   8   9   10   11   12   13   ★

Great! Now players can set traps to defeat the vampire pizzas in your game! In this chapter, you used what you know about things like classes, conditionals, and loops to make all the pieces of your game fit together!

Chapter 13
Win and Lose Conditions

We're almost done! All the individual parts of our game work, but our game never ends! In this chapter, we will set up some **win** and **lose** conditions for the game.

Lose Condition: Players lose if three vampire pizzas make it into their pizza boxes.

Win Condition: Players win if they can hold out for three minutes without allowing three vampire pizzas into their pizza boxes.

To set these conditions, we need:

1. The ability to count how many vampire pizzas have gotten into the boxes.

2. A timer that will count the three minutes.

3. A message for the player, letting them know if they've won or lost the game.

PLAN
BUILD
TEST

Counting Pizzas

Throughout the game, a player cannot let vampire pizzas reach their delivery boxes. When a vampire pizza makes it into a delivery box, the angry customer will leave a terrible review. Get three terrible reviews and the whole restaurant will be shut down!

In game terms, the player will start with zero bad reviews, and every time a vampire pizza reaches a delivery box, one bad review will be added to the player's total. When the total reaches three, the game will end.

Counting Time

If the player's bad review total does not reach three by the time the game timer counts to three minutes, the player has won and the game will end. The timer that we set up will count down from 180 **seconds** (3 minutes).

Set Up Variables

Let's set up the bad-review count and the game timer. We'll create a variable that contains the maximum number of bad reviews that a player can get. Then we'll create a variable that contains the total time a player has to survive to win the game.

>>> **Type This**

```
#Set up counters
STARTING_BUCKS = 15
BUCK_RATE = 120
STARTING_BUCK_BOOSTER = 1

#Set up win/lose conditions
MAX_BAD_REVIEWS = 3
WIN_TIME = FRAME_RATE * 60 * 3

#Define speeds
REG_SPEED = 2
SLOW_SPEED = 1
```

BUILD
PLAN
TEST

How long is the WIN_TIME ?

As you know, the frame rate is how many times the game loop runs per second. The frame rate multiplied by 60 gives us the number of times the game loop runs in 1 minute. The frame rate multiplied by 60 then by 3 gives us the number of times the game loop runs in 3 minutes. If you want to change the win time later on, just change the 3 to the number of minutes that you want the game to last.

Set Up Attributes

We will need to count both the number of bad reviews and the amount of time passing. We'll add both of these to the **Counters** class.

>>> **Type This**

```
class Counters(object):
    def __init__(self, pizza_bucks, buck_rate, buck_booster):
    def __init__(self, pizza_bucks, buck_rate,
                    buck_booster, timer)
        self.loop_count = 0
        self.display_font = font.Font('pizza_font.ttf', 25)
        self.pizza_bucks = pizza_bucks
        self.buck_rate = buck_rate
        self.buck_booster = buck_booster
        self.bucks_rect = None
        self.timer = timer
        self.timer_rect = None

    def increment_bucks(self):
        if self.loop_count % self.buck_rate == 0:
            self.pizza_bucks += self.buck_booster
```

Take a Closer Look

```
class Counters(object):
    def __init__(self, pizza_bucks, buck_rate,
                 buck_booster, timer)
        self.loop_count = 0
        self.display_font = font.Font('pizza_font.ttf', 25)
        self.pizza_bucks = pizza_bucks
        self.buck_rate = buck_rate
        self.buck_booster = buck_booster
        self.bucks_rect = None
        self.timer = timer
        self.timer_rect = None
```

```
def __init__(self, pizza_bucks, buck_rate,
             buck_booster, timer):
```

First we added one argument to the method: **timer**.

```
class Counters(object):
    def __init__(self, pizza_bucks, buck_rate,
                 buck_booster, timer)
        self.loop_count = 0
        self.display_font = font.Font('pizza_font.ttf', 25)
        self.pizza_bucks = pizza_bucks
        self.buck_rate = buck_rate
        self.buck_booster = buck_booster
        self.bucks_rect = None
        self.timer = timer
        self.timer_rect = None
```

```
self.timer = timer
self.timer_rect = None
```

Then we created two new attributes called **timer** and **timer_rect**.

Your Turn

Next, we'll set up the count of bad reviews.

```
#Counters class, init method
    self.buck_booster = buck_booster
    self.bucks_rect = None
    self.timer = timer
    self.timer_rect = None
#To do: Add bad_reviews attribute here
#To do: Add bad_reviews_rect attribute here

    def increment_bucks(self):
        if self.loop_count % self.buck_rate == 0:
            self.pizza_bucks += self.buck_booster
```

1. Create an attribute called `bad_reviews` and set the value to `0`.

2. Create an attribute called `bad_rev_rect` and set the value to `None`.

Count Reviews

Every time we update the vampire pizzas, we want to check whether they've touched a delivery box and add `1` to `bad_reviews` if they have.

>>> **Type This**

```
#VampireSprite class
    def update(self, game_window, counters):
        game_window.blit(BACKGROUND, (self.rect.x,
                        self.rect.y), self.rect)
        self.rect.x -= self.speed
        if self.health <= 0 or self.rect.x <= 100:
            self.kill()
            if self.rect.x <= 100:
                counters.bad_reviews += 1
        else:
            game_window.blit(self.image, (self.rect.x, self.rect.y))

    def attack(self, tile):
```

Display Score

The player can see how many pizza bucks they have. We also want to display the number of bad reviews and the timer, so players can keep track of how they're doing in the game. We'll add the reviews display together, and then you'll add the timer display on your own.

```
#Counters class, draw_bucks method
        self.bucks_rect.x = WINDOW_WIDTH - 50
        self.bucks_rect.y = WINDOW_HEIGHT - 50
        game_window.blit(bucks_surf, self.bucks_rect)

#Draw the player's bad reviews total to the screen
    def draw_bad_reviews(self, game_window):
#Test if there is a new number of bad reviews and erase the
#old number if there is
        if bool(self.bad_rev_rect):
            game_window.blit(BACKGROUND, (self.bad_rev_rect.x,
                    self.bad_rev_rect.y), self.bad_rev_rect)
#Tell the program the font and color to use in the display
        bad_rev_surf = self.display_font.render(
                    str(self.bad_reviews), True, WHITE)
#Set up a rect so that we can interact with the number
        self.bad_rev_rect = bad_rev_surf.get_rect()
#Put the display in the second-to-last column and bottom
#row of the grid
        self.bad_rev_rect.x = WINDOW_WIDTH - 150
        self.bad_rev_rect.y = WINDOW_HEIGHT - 50
#Display the number to the screen
        game_window.blit(bad_rev_surf, self.bad_rev_rect)

#To Do: Define the method draw_time here
#To Do: Test for a new time
#To Do: Erase the old time if there's a new one
#To Do: Tell the program the font and color for the display
#To Do: Set up a rect
#To Do: Tell the program which column to put the display in
#To Do: Tell the program which row to put the display in
#To Do: Display the time to the screen

    def update(self, game_window):
        self.loop_count += 1
        self.increment_bucks()
```

 **Your Turn**

Notice how similar this is to the `draw_bucks` method. On your own, you'll use the same pattern from `draw_bucks` and `draw_bad_reviews` to create the method that draws the timer.

1. Call the method `draw_timer`.

2. To display the timer in seconds, use the equation
   `WIN_TIME - self.loop_count // FRAME_RATE`

3. Place the timer display in the bottom row, three columns from the right.

Check Your Work

```
#Counters class
    def draw_timer(self, game_window):
        if bool(self.timer_rect):
            game_window.blit(BACKGROUND, (self.timer_rect.x,
                                self.timer_rect.y), self.timer_rect)
        timer_surf = self.display_font.render(str(
            (WIN_TIME - self.loop_count) // FRAME_RATE), True, WHITE)
        self.timer_rect = timer_surf.get_rect()
        self.timer_rect.x = WINDOW_WIDTH - 250
        self.timer_rect.y = WINDOW_HEIGHT - 50
        game_window.blit(timer_surf, self.timer_rect)


    def update(self, game_window):
        self.loop_count += 1
        self.increment_bucks()
```

Call the Methods

Let's use the Counters class update method to call our two new methods.

```
#Counters class
    def update(self, game_window):
        self.loop_count += 1
        self.increment_bucks()
        self.draw_bucks(game_window)
        self.draw_bad_reviews(game_window)
#To Do: Call the draw_timer method here

class Trap(object):
    def __init__(self, trap_kind, cost, trap_img):
        self.trap_kind = trap_kind
```

▶ **Your Turn**

1. Call the method `draw_time`.

2. Pass in the `game_window` when you call the method.

End-of-Game Message

Now, if either the **win** or **lose** condition is met, the game window will automatically close. But we want to tell the player how they did! So we'll display an end-of-game message. In order to show a message after the gameplay has stopped, we need to create another loop that runs after the game loop is done. To make this work, we need to add a variable called `program_running`.

```
                    draw.rect(BACKGROUND, tile_color, (WIDTH * column,
                          HEIGHT * row, WIDTH, HEIGHT), 1)

GAME_WINDOW.blit(BACKGROUND, (0,0))

#------------------------------------------------
#Game loop

#Define the conditions for running the loop
game_running = True
program_running = True

#Start game loop
while game_running:

    for event in pygame.event.get():

        if event.type == QUIT:
            game_running = False
            program_running = False

        elif event.type == MOUSEBUTTONDOWN:
            coordinates = mouse.get_pos()
            x = coordinates [0]
            y = coordinates [1]
```

When `game_running` is set to `False` and `program_running` is set to `True`, it will run our end-of-game loop with our end-of-game message. When the player meets either the **win** condition or the **lose** condition, we will change the value of `game_running` to `False`.

Your Turn

```python
        if bool(left_tile):
            vampire.attack(left_tile)
        if bool(right_tile):
            if right_tile != left_tile:
                vampire.attack(right_tile)


        #---------------------------
        #Set win/lose conditions
        #To Do: Test for the lose condition here
        #To Do: If the player lost set game_running to False
        #To Do: Test for the win condition here
        #To Do: If the player won set game_running to False


        #---------------------------
        #Update displays
        for vampire in all_vampires:
            vampire.update(GAME_WINDOW, counters)
```

First we'll test for the **lose** condition:

1. Test if `counters.bad_reviews` is greater than or equal to `MAX_BAD_REVIEWS`.

2. If True, change `game_running` to `False`.

Now we'll test for the **win** condition:

3. Test if `counters.loop_count` is greater than `WIN_TIME`.

4. If True, change `game_running` to `False`.

```
            if bool(left_tile):
                vampire.attack(left_tile)
            if bool(right_tile):
                if right_tile != left_tile:
                    vampire.attack(right_tile)

        #-----------------------------
        #Set win/lose conditions
        if counters.bad_reviews >= MAX_BAD_REVIEWS:
            game_running = False

        if counters.loop_count > WIN_TIME:
            game_running = False

    #-----------------------------------
    #Update displays
        for vampire in all_vampires:
            vampire.update(GAME_WINDOW, counters)
```

Display Message

The last part to add is the end-of-game loop that will display
our message to the player.

>>> **Type This**

```
        counters.update(GAME_WINDOW)
        display.update()
        clock.tick(FRAME_RATE)

#Close main game loop
#------------------------------------------------------------
#Set up the font
end_font = font.Font('pizza_font.ttf', 50)
#Test if either the win or lose condition has been met
if program_running:
#To Do: Test for lose condition here
#To Do: Render the lose message here
#To Do: Else
#To Do: Render the win message here
#To Do: Blit the end message to the screen
    display.update()
```

```
#------------------------------------------
#Start end-of-game loop
while program_running:
    for event in pygame.event.get():
#Listen for the QUIT event
        if event.type == QUIT:
            program_running = False
#Set the frame rate
    clock.tick(FRAME_RATE)

#------------------------------------------
#Close end-of-game loop

#Clean up game
pygame.quit()
```

 **Your Turn**

To display the messages, we'll use a method called `render()`. Render creates a new surface that is the text. Render takes 3 arguments: the text of the message, turn **antialiasings** on or off, and the color.

Antialiasing is a technique to smooth out the jaggedness of digital graphics.

1. Test for the lose condition: `bad_reviews` greater than or equal to `MAX_BAD_REVIEWS`.

2. If True, call the method `render()` on `end_font`. Pass it three arguments: `'Game Over'`, `True`, and `WHITE`.

3. Store the whole method in a variable called `end_surf`.

The render method should look like this:

`end_surf = end_font.render('Game Over', True, WHITE)`

4. **else** if the test is False.

5. Call the method **render()** on **end_font**. Pass it the arguments: **'You Win!'**, **True**, and **WHITE**.

6. Store the method in a variable called **end_surf**.

7. Use **blit** to display **end_surf** to the **GAME_WINDOW** at **(350, 200)**.

Check Your Work

```
#Set end-of-game message
end_font = font.Font('pizza_font.ttf', 50)

if program_running:
    if counters.bad_reviews >= MAX_BAD_REVIEWS:
        end_surf = end_font.render('Game Over', True, WHITE)
    else:
        end_surf = end_font.render('You Win!', True, WHITE)
    GAME_WINDOW.blit(end_surf, (350, 200))
    display.update()
```

You're almost there! The last step is debugging the program until it works.

Run Your Code

Make sure to run your code. Play through the game several times to make sure it runs in all different situations. If you find errors, stop and debug your code.

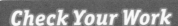

Code for *Attack of the Vampire Pizzas!*

This is the complete game code. You can use it to check your work. If you are looking at this code while working on an earlier chapter, it may look different than the code you are working on because you will change some of the code you write as you progress through the game. You can download this file on the *Code This Game* website, **OddDot.com/codethisgame**.

```python
#Game set up

#Import libraries
import pygame
from pygame import *
from random import randint

#Initialize pygame
pygame.init()

#Set up the clock
clock = time.Clock()

#-----------------------------------------------
#Define constant variables

#Define game window parameters
WINDOW_WIDTH = 1100
WINDOW_HEIGHT = 600
WINDOW_RES = (WINDOW_WIDTH, WINDOW_HEIGHT)

#Define tile parameters
WIDTH = 100
HEIGHT = 100

#Define colors
WHITE = (255, 255, 255)

#Set up rates
SPAWN_RATE = 360
FRAME_RATE = 60

#Set up counters
STARTING_BUCKS = 15
```

```python
BUCK_RATE = 120
STARTING_BUCK_BOOSTER = 1

#Set up win/lose conditions
MAX_BAD_REVIEWS = 3
WIN_TIME = FRAME_RATE * 60 * 3

#Define speeds
REG_SPEED = 2
SLOW_SPEED = 1


#---------------------------------------------
#Load assets

#Create the game window
GAME_WINDOW = display.set_mode(WINDOW_RES)
display.set_caption('Attack of the Vampire Pizzas!')

#Set up the background image
background_img = image.load('restaurant.jpg')
background_surf = Surface.convert_alpha(background_img)
BACKGROUND = transform.scale(background_surf, WINDOW_RES)

#Set up the enemy image
pizza_img = image.load('vampire.png')
pizza_surf = Surface.convert_alpha(pizza_img)
VAMPIRE_PIZZA = transform.scale(pizza_surf, (WIDTH, HEIGHT))

#Set up the trap images
garlic_img = image.load('garlic.png')
garlic_surf = Surface.convert_alpha(garlic_img)
GARLIC = transform.scale(garlic_surf, (WIDTH, HEIGHT))

cutter_img = image.load('pizzacutter.png')
cutter_surf = Surface.convert_alpha(cutter_img)
CUTTER = transform.scale(cutter_surf, (WIDTH, HEIGHT))

pepperoni_img = image.load('pepperoni.png')
pepperoni_surf = Surface.convert_alpha(pepperoni_img)
PEPPERONI = transform.scale(pepperoni_surf, (WIDTH, HEIGHT))

#---------------------------------------------
#Set up class objects

#Create an enemy object
class VampireSprite(sprite.Sprite):
```

```python
        #Set up enemy instances
        def __init__(self):
            super().__init__()
            self.speed = REG_SPEED
            self.lane = randint(0, 4)
            all_vampires.add(self)
            self.image = VAMPIRE_PIZZA.copy()
            y = 50 + self.lane * 100
            self.rect = self.image.get_rect(center = (1100, y))
            self.health = 100

        #Set up enemy movement
        def update(self, game_window, counters):
            game_window.blit(BACKGROUND,
                             (self.rect.x, self.rect.y), self.rect)
            self.rect.x -= self.speed
            if self.health <= 0 or self.rect.x <= 100:
                self.kill()
                if self.rect.x <= 100:
                    counters.bad_reviews += 1
            else:
                game_window.blit(self.image, (self.rect.x, self.rect.y))

        #Apply trap effects to enemies
        def attack(self, tile):
            if tile.trap == SLOW:
                self.speed = SLOW_SPEED
            if tile.trap == DAMAGE:
                self.health -= 1

#Create an object for tracking the game state
class Counters(object):

        #Set up instances of counters
        def __init__(self, pizza_bucks, buck_rate,
                     buck_booster, timer):
            self.loop_count = 0
            self.display_font = font.Font('pizza_font.ttf', 25)
            self.pizza_bucks = pizza_bucks
            self.buck_rate = buck_rate
            self.buck_booster = buck_booster
            self.bucks_rect = None
            self.timer = timer
            self.timer_rect = None
```

```python
    self.bad_reviews = 0
    self.bad_rev_rect = None

#Set the rate that the player earns pizza bucks
def increment_bucks(self):
    if self.loop_count % self.buck_rate == 0:
        self.pizza_bucks += self.buck_booster

#Display pizza bucks total on the screen
def draw_bucks(self, game_window):
    if bool(self.bucks_rect):
        game_window.blit(BACKGROUND, (self.bucks_rect.x,
                            self.bucks_rect.y), self.bucks_rect)
    bucks_surf = self.display_font.render(
                        str(self.pizza_bucks), True, WHITE)
    self.bucks_rect = bucks_surf.get_rect()
    self.bucks_rect.x = WINDOW_WIDTH - 50
    self.bucks_rect.y = WINDOW_HEIGHT - 50
    game_window.blit(bucks_surf, self.bucks_rect)

#Display bad reviews total on the screen
def draw_bad_reviews(self, game_window):
    if bool(self.bad_rev_rect):
        game_window.blit(BACKGROUND, (self.bad_rev_rect.x,
                        self.bad_rev_rect.y), self.bad_rev_rect)
    bad_rev_surf = self.display_font.render(
                        str(self.bad_reviews), True, WHITE)
    self.bad_rev_rect = bad_rev_surf.get_rect()
    self.bad_rev_rect.x = WINDOW_WIDTH - 150
    self.bad_rev_rect.y = WINDOW_HEIGHT - 50
    game_window.blit(bad_rev_surf, self.bad_rev_rect)

#Display time remaining on the screen
def draw_timer(self, game_window):
    if bool(self.timer_rect):
        game_window.blit(BACKGROUND, (self.timer_rect.x,
                            self.timer_rect.y), self.timer_rect)
    timer_surf = self.display_font.render(str(
        (WIN_TIME - self.loop_count) // FRAME_RATE), True, WHITE)
    self.timer_rect = timer_surf.get_rect()
    self.timer_rect.x = WINDOW_WIDTH - 250
    self.timer_rect.y = WINDOW_HEIGHT - 50
    game_window.blit(timer_surf, self.timer_rect)
```

```python
    #Increment the loop_counter and call the other Counters
    #methods
    def update(self, game_window):
        self.loop_count += 1
        self.increment_bucks()
        self.draw_bucks(game_window)
        self.draw_bad_reviews(game_window)
        self.draw_timer(game_window)

#Create a trap object
class Trap(object):

    #Set up instances of each kind of trap
    def __init__(self, trap_kind, cost, trap_img):
        self.trap_kind = trap_kind
        self.cost = cost
        self.trap_img = trap_img

#Create an object that activates traps
class TrapApplicator(object):

    #Set up TrapApplicator instances
    def __init__(self):
        self.selected = None

    #Activate a trap button
    def select_trap(self, trap):
        if trap.cost <= counters.pizza_bucks:
            self.selected = trap

    #Lay a trap on a specific tile
    def select_tile(self, tile, counters):
        self.selected = tile.set_trap(self.selected, counters)

#Create a background tile object
class BackgroundTile(sprite.Sprite):

    #Set up instances of background tiles
    def __init__(self, rect):
        super().__init__()
        self.trap = None
        self.rect = rect

#Create a subclass for tiles in the play area
class PlayTile(BackgroundTile):
```

```python
    #Lay traps on tiles in the play area
    def set_trap(self, trap, counters):
        if bool(trap) and not bool(self.trap):
            counters.pizza_bucks -= trap.cost
            self.trap = trap
            if trap == EARN:
                counters.buck_booster += 1
        return None

    #Display trap images on tiles in the play area
    def draw_trap(self, game_window, trap_applicator):
        if bool(self.trap):
            game_window.blit(self.trap.trap_img,
                            (self.rect.x, self.rect.y))

#Create a subclass for tiles that are trap buttons
class ButtonTile(BackgroundTile):

    #Click on a trap button to select the trap
    def set_trap(self, trap, counters):
        if counters.pizza_bucks >= self.trap.cost:
            return self.trap
        else:
            return None

    #Highlight the trap button that was clicked
    def draw_trap(self, game_window, trap_applicator):
        if bool(trap_applicator.selected):
            if trap_applicator.selected == self.trap:
                draw.rect(game_window, (238, 190, 47),
                        (self.rect.x, self.rect.y, WIDTH, HEIGHT), 5)

#Create a subclass for tiles that are not interactive
class InactiveTile(BackgroundTile):

    #Do nothing if clicked
    def set_trap(self, trap, counters):
        return None

    #Do not display anything
    def draw_trap(self, game_window, trap_applicator):
        pass

#------------------------------------------------------------
#Create class instances and groups
```

```python
#Create a group for all VampireSprite instances
all_vampires = sprite.Group()

#Create an instance of Counters
counters = Counters(STARTING_BUCKS, BUCK_RATE,
                    STARTING_BUCK_BOOSTER, WIN_TIME)

#Create instances of each kind of trap
SLOW = Trap('SLOW', 5, GARLIC)
DAMAGE = Trap('DAMAGE', 3, CUTTER)
EARN = Trap('EARN', 7, PEPPERONI)

#Create an instance of the TrapApplicator
trap_applicator = TrapApplicator()

#------------------------------------------------
#Initialize and draw the background grid

#Create an empty list to hold tile grid
tile_grid = []
#Define the color of the grid outline
tile_color = WHITE

#Populate the background grid
for row in range(6):
    row_of_tiles = []
    tile_grid.append(row_of_tiles)
    for column in range(11):
        tile_rect = Rect(WIDTH * column, HEIGHT * row,
                         WIDTH, HEIGHT)
        if column <= 1:
            new_tile = InactiveTile(tile_rect)
        else:
            if row == 5:
                if 2 <= column <= 4:
                    new_tile = ButtonTile(tile_rect)
                    new_tile.trap = [SLOW, DAMAGE, EARN][column - 2]
                else:
                    new_tile = InactiveTile(tile_rect)
            else:
                new_tile = PlayTile(tile_rect)
        row_of_tiles.append(new_tile)
        if row == 5 and 2 <= column <= 4:
            BACKGROUND.blit(new_tile.trap.trap_img,
                            (new_tile.rect.x, new_tile.rect.y))
```

```python
        if column != 0 and row != 5:
            if column != 1:
                draw.rect(BACKGROUND, tile_color, (WIDTH * column,
                          HEIGHT * row, WIDTH, HEIGHT), 1)

#Display the background image to the screen
GAME_WINDOW.blit(BACKGROUND, (0,0))

#--------------------------------------------------
#Game loop

#Define the conditions for running the loop
game_running = True
program_running = True

#Start game loop
while game_running:

    #--------------------------
    #Check for events

    #Start loop to check for and handle events
    for event in pygame.event.get():
        #Exit the loop when the game window closes
        if event.type == QUIT:
            game_running = False
            program_running = False
        #Set up the background tiles to respond to mouse clicks
        elif event.type == MOUSEBUTTONDOWN:
            coordinates = mouse.get_pos()
            x = coordinates[0]
            y = coordinates[1]
            tile_y = y // 100
            tile_x = x // 100
            trap_applicator.select_tile(
                          tile_grid[tile_y][tile_x], counters)

    #--------------------------
    #Spawn sprites

    #Spawn vampire pizza sprites
    if randint(1, SPAWN_RATE) == 1:
        VampireSprite()
```

```python
#------------------------
#Set up collision detection

#Draw the background grid
for tile_row in tile_grid:
    for tile in tile_row:
        if bool(tile.trap):
            GAME_WINDOW.blit(BACKGROUND, (tile.rect.x,
                             tile.rect.y), tile.rect)


#Set up detection for collision with background tiles
for vampire in all_vampires:
    tile_row = tile_grid[vampire.rect.y // 100]
    vamp_left_side = vampire.rect.x // 100
    vamp_right_side = (vampire.rect.x +
                       vampire.rect.width) // 100
    if 0 <= vamp_left_side <= 10:
        left_tile = tile_row[vamp_left_side]
    else:
        left_tile = None
    if 0 <= vamp_right_side <= 10:
        right_tile = tile_row[vamp_right_side]
    else:
        right_tile = None

    if bool(left_tile):
        vampire.attack(left_tile)
    if bool(right_tile):
        if right_tile != left_tile:
            vampire.attack(right_tile)

#------------------------
#Set win/lose conditions

#Test for lose condition
if counters.bad_reviews >= MAX_BAD_REVIEWS:
    game_running = False
#Test for win condition
if counters.loop_count > WIN_TIME:
    game_running = False

#------------------------
#Update displays
```

```
    #Update enemies
    for vampire in all_vampires:
        vampire.update(GAME_WINDOW, counters)

    #Update traps that have been set
    for tile_row in tile_grid:
        for tile in tile_row:
            tile.draw_trap(GAME_WINDOW, trap_applicator)

    #Update counters
    counters.update(GAME_WINDOW)

    #Update all images on the screen
    display.update()

    #Set the frame rate
    clock.tick(FRAME_RATE)

#-----------------------------------------------
#Close main game loop

#Set up end game messages
end_font = font.Font('pizza_font.ttf', 50)
if program_running:
    if counters.bad_reviews >= MAX_BAD_REVIEWS:
            end_surf = end_font.render('Game Over', True, WHITE)
    else:
            end_surf = end_font.render('You Win!', True, WHITE)
    GAME_WINDOW.blit(end_surf, (350, 200))
    display.update()

#Enable exit from end game message screen
while program_running:
    for event in pygame.event.get():
        if event.type == QUIT:
            program_running = False
    clock.tick(FRAME_RATE)

#-----------------------------------------------
#Close end game message loop

#Clean up the game
pygame.quit()
```

Level Up!

0 1 2 3 4 5 6 7 8 9 10 11 12 **13** ★

Congratulations! You have programmed an entire
video game and learned the basics of coding in Python!
To get to this level, you had to problem-solve, be
persistent, and work hard on your coding skills!
Check out the bonus levels in Part 3!

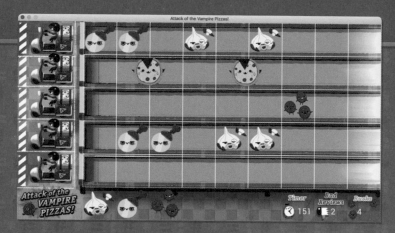

**YOU DID IT!
You made**
*Attack of
the Vampire
Pizzas!*

In the next part, we'll explore how to customize, mod, and hack
the game! You can even use the assets to create new games all
your own. But before you can do any of that, you have to . . .

Part 3:
Break This Game

Chapter 14

Customize Your Game

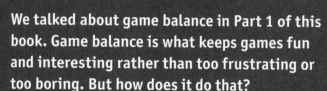

Balance

We talked about game balance in Part 1 of this book. Game balance is what keeps games fun and interesting rather than too frustrating or too boring. But how does it do that?

How Does Game Balance Work?

Playing games is about making interesting choices. If the player's choices don't matter, the game is not balanced. If a game is too hard, the player's choices don't matter because they almost always lose. If there is only one solution to a game, the player's choices don't matter because they only need to find that one solution to always win the game. Let's think about a couple of examples.

Imagine we are going to add a new trap to our game. This trap costs zero pizza bucks and stays in place until the end of the game. It immediately destroys all vampire pizzas that it touches. With this new trap, you could always quickly win the game. Would this trap make the game more fun? Does this trap encourage the player to make interesting choices?

When we think about this trap, we can see that it clearly ruins the balance of the game. All the player has to do to win is place five of these new traps, one for each row, then just sit back and wait for the timer to hit three minutes. For a player trying to win the game, there is no other choice.

Because this new trap is free, there are no trade-offs. One way to ensure balance is to make sure that your game components have trade-offs. For example, a very powerful trap might cost a higher amount of pizza bucks, while a weaker trap costs a lower amount of pizza bucks. Then the player has to choose between saving pizza bucks for a more powerful trap or laying as many weaker traps as they can.

Balancing your game is part of the art of creating digital games. There is no single right answer, and there is no math problem that can balance your game for you. (Though there are some math problems that might help!) There is no test that can tell you if your game is balanced. You will use your own preferences and judgment to decide if your game is balanced. The basic strategy that you will use to balance your game is to make your best guess, play your game, then make adjustments based on playing the game.

It's usually easier to tell if something is unbalanced. Ask yourself: What is too high, and what is too low? For example, at what speed is the game too fast? At what speed is it too slow? Pick a speed somewhere in between. At what amount does a trap cost too much? What about too little? Pick an amount in between. Once you have your starting numbers, playtest your game. It is important that other people besides you playtest your game. The best way to playtest is to find as many different play-testers as you can.

For example, a professional game designer would want all types of people testing their game, players of all genders, players of different ages, players from different ethnic or cultural backgrounds, players that enjoy different types of games and have different play styles. Game designers get feedback about many elements of their game from play-testers, including the balance of the game.

Balancing Vampire Pizzas

Now it's your turn to balance *Attack of the Vampire Pizzas!* In general, balancing is usually about making changes to the numbers. Let's think about what numbers in our game might affect balance.

The number of vampire pizzas that can reach the boxes before the player loses

The rate that pizza bucks are earned over time

The amount of time on the timer

The rate at which hit points are lost from the damage trap

The number of hit points the vampire pizzas start with

The impact on speed from the slow trap

The rate that vampire pizzas are spawned

The speed at which the vampire pizzas move

The rate at which pizza bucks increase from the earn trap

Think of your game as a complex web. Any adjustment that you make to one part of the game will affect the other parts. So if you adjust one number, you might end up needing to adjust other game elements as well.

Power Up: *As you make adjustments to your game, it is important to keep data types in mind. Data types don't mix and match. If you are rebalancing something that used an integer (a whole number), you will need to change it to another integer. If you use a float (a number with a decimal in it), it could create a bug in your game.*

Create a New File

Before you start to play around with your code, be sure to create a new file. This way you will have a copy of the original game to go back to. Create a file by clicking **File** then **Save As**. Save your new file in the same directory as your game file. Call it **VampirePizzaCustomized.py**.

Adjusting Spawn Rate

Start by adjusting the spawn rate of the vampire pizzas. Spawning pizzas more frequently will increase the challenge of the game. Spawning pizzas less frequently will decrease the challenge of the game.

We have the variable **SPAWN_RATE** set to 360. This means that a vampire pizza has a 1 in 360 chance of spawning during each game loop.

 **Your Turn**

```
WIDTH = 100
HEIGHT = 100

WHITE = (255, 255, 255)

SPAWN_RATE = 360
FRAME_RATE = 60
STARTING_BUCKS = 15
BUCK_RATE = 120
```

1. Change 360 to a bigger number. Then run and play the game.

2. Now change 360 to a smaller number. Then run and play the game.

With each test, ask yourself: What changed? Did you enjoy the gameplay?

As you test the game, can you find the limits? What number is definitely too hard? What number is definitely too easy? Try a number in the middle.

Test the game as many times as you want until you find the just-right spawn rate for your game.

Adjust Pizza Bucks

Now try adjusting the amount of pizza bucks. Starting with more pizza bucks or earning them faster will make the game easier.

Starting with fewer pizza bucks or earning them slower will make the game more difficult. **STARTING_BUCKS** is set to **15**. This means that players start the game with 15 pizza bucks. **BUCK_RATE** is set to **120**. This means that every 120 game loops, the player will earn 1 pizza buck.

```
WHITE = (255, 255, 255)

SPAWN_RATE = 360
FRAME_RATE = 60
STARTING_BUCKS = 15
BUCK_RATE = 120
STARTING_BUCK_BOOSTER = 1
MAX_BAD_REVIEWS = 3
WIN_TIME = FRAME_RATE * 60 * 3

REG_SPEED = 2
SLOW_SPEED = 1
```

▶ Your Turn

1. Increase the amount of pizza bucks that a player starts with and lower the rate that bucks are earned. Then run and play the game. How did the changes you made affect gameplay?

2. Try at least two more combinations of **STARTING_BUCKS** and **BUCK_RATE** until you find the challenge level that you like best.

Adjust Traps

You can change both the cost of each trap and the effect that each trap has. Creating balanced traps is about trade-offs for the player. In general, the more powerful a trap is, the more pizza bucks it should cost. Start by making changes to the **damage** trap.

Find the attack method in the **VampireSprite** class.

```
#VampireSprite class
    def attack(self, tile):
        if tile.trap == SLOW:
            self.speed = SLOW_SPEED
        if tile.trap == DAMAGE:
            self.health -= 1

class Counters(object):

    def __init__(self, pizza_bucks, buck_rate, buck_booster, timer):
```

Right now, vampire sprites lose **1** point of health each game loop after they touch a damage trap. You can change the number of health points that they lose by changing the number 1. It is important not to change the data type. 1 is an integer (it does not have a decimal in it). Make sure to only change the 1 to other integers (whole numbers).

You can also change the cost of the trap by scrolling down to where the **DAMAGE** trap is initiated and changing the second argument, which is currently a **3**. This means that it costs 3 pizza bucks to purchase the damage trap.

```
counters = Counters(STARTING_BUCKS, BUCK_RATE,
                    STARTING_BUCK_BOOSTER, WIN_TIME)

SLOW = Trap('SLOW', 5, GARLIC)
DAMAGE = Trap('DAMAGE', 3, CUTTER)
EARN = Trap('EARN', 7, PEPPERONI)

trap_applicator = TrapApplicator()
```

▶ Your Turn

1. Try making the trap much more powerful by doing more damage. When you do this, increase the cost of the trap. Run and play the game.

2. Try making the trap much less powerful by doing less damage. To do this, you will have to increase the amount of health that the vampire pizzas start with, since 1 is the least you can take away. You can do this in the **init** method of the **VampireSprite** class. Decrease the cost of the trap. Run and play the game.

Make adjustments to the damage trap until you feel that it is just right. Remember, each part of the game affects all the other parts, so after you adjust the damage trap, you may want to go back and tinker with the rate that pizza bucks are earned or the rate that vampire pizzas are spawned.

Power Up: Test only one change at a time. It will be easier to fix if one of your changes breaks the game.

Making Other Adjustments

Now use your imagination. What other adjustments can you make to the balance without changing any of the core game mechanics? Do you want to adjust the win or lose conditions? What about the speed at which the vampire pizzas move? What other numbers-based changes can you think of?

 **Your Turn**

Go ahead and make the changes that you want. Run and test the game after each change.

If you run into a bug, think about if there are other parts of the game that interact with the part that you changed. You may need to change more than one number to get the effect that you want.

Theme

You can also change the theme of a game without altering the way that the game plays. You can do this by swapping out the assets. We'll change the theme to *Alien Invasion* together. Then you can pick a different theme based on your own preferences. Start by creating a copy of your game.

As you make changes and additions to the game, always use **Save As** to make a new copy of the game file to work in. It's important to be free to experiment, play around with different ideas, and make mistakes. If you have your working game saved in another file, you can break your game (and fix it again) without fear!

We'll start by changing the name of the game.

```
GAME_WINDOW = display.set_mode(WINDOW_RES)
- display.set_caption('Attack of the Vampire Pizzas!')
+ display.set_caption('Alien Invasion')
```

Then change the game images.

```
background_img = image.load('restaurant.jpg')
background_img = image.load('galaxy.jpg')
background_surf = Surface.convert(background_img)
BACKGROUND = transform.scale(background_surf, WINDOW_RES)
```

Your Turn

Now it's your turn. Select one of the **aliens**. Find the image of the vampire pizza in your code and change the file name.

Find the images of the traps in your code: **garlic**, **pizza cutter**, and **pepperoni**. Think about what the traps might be in space. For example, if you select the **meteor** to do damage and stop the alien, then you would change the pizza cutter image to the image of the meteor. For the space traps, you can select from **meteor**, **wormhole**, and **stars**.

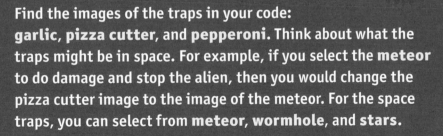

When you are done, run your game to make sure that all the assets work and to try out your new theme!

Can you create your own mix-and-match theme?

Adding Your Own Assets

You can also choose to use your own assets. If you like to draw or do digital design, you can create your own images. Save the images as **.jpg** or **.png** files in your game directory. I recommend creating the images at the resolution that you plan to use in the game.

You can also find images online. If you plan to share your game, make sure to check the usage rights of the images that you find. You can filter an image search based on images licensed for reuse. You can also search for images that have a Creative Commons license. You are free to use any of the *Code This Game!* assets in any way that you'd like.

Save **.jpg** or **.png** images that you want to use in your game directory. For the best look, try to find images that are multiples of the resolution that you plan to use in the game.

Chapter 15

Mod Your Game

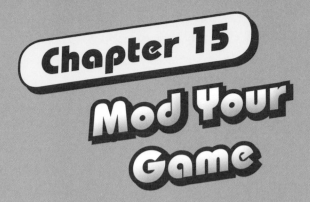

> You can also add new features to your game. In this chapter, you will learn how to add two new features to your game:
>
> 1. Changing the look of a sprite.
>
> 2. Adding new enemy types.

Remember to use **Save As** to create a new file for each mod so that you don't lose any of your past work.

Change the Look of a Sprite

The first mod we'll create will change the look of the vampire pizza sprite. When the vampire pizza hits a pizza cutter trap, it loses health points over time. As the vampire pizza loses health points, we can make it look sicker and sicker.

The vampire pizza sprite starts with **100** health points. We will change the image of the sprite when it reaches **60** points and again when it reaches **30** points.

Player Feedback

Changing the image of the vampire sprite to indicate how many health points it has lost is one way to provide player feedback. **Player feedback** is any type of image, sound, or text that gives the player information that they can use to play the game.

Changing the vampire pizza image based on health points is an example of visual feedback. The player can see the rate at which the vampire pizza is losing health points by looking at the sprite image. The player can use this information to decide if they need to place an additional trap or if the vampire pizza will be destroyed before reaching the pizza boxes.

Another example of player feedback in the game is our counter displays on the bottom-right corner of the game window. These are examples of text feedback. The displays tell the player how many pizza bucks they currently have, how many bad reviews they have accumulated, and how much time has passed in the game.

>>> **Type This**

```
#Set up counters
STARTING_BUCKS = 15
BUCK_RATE = 120
STARTING_BUCK_BOOSTER = 1
STARTING_HEALTH = 100

#Set up win/lose conditions
MAX_BAD_REVIEWS = 3
WIN_TIME = FRAME_RATE * 60 * 3
```

Here is the code for setting up the image **'pizza60health.png'**. Add this code to your program. Then use the same pattern to set up **'pizza30health.png'**.

```
pizza_img = image.load('vampire.png')
pizza_surf = Surface.convert_alpha(pizza_img)
VAMPIRE_PIZZA = transform.scale(pizza_surf, (WIDTH, HEIGHT))

med_health_img = image.load('pizza60health.png')
med_health_surf = Surface.convert_alpha(med_health_img)
MED_HEALTH = transform.scale(med_health_surf, (WIDTH, HEIGHT))

#To Do: Load 'pizza30health.png' here
#To Do: Convert it to a surface
#To Do: Set the size of LOW_HEALTH here

garlic_img = image.load('garlic.png')
garlic_surf = Surface.convert_alpha(garlic_img)
GARLIC = transform.scale(garlic_surf, (WIDTH, HEIGHT))
```

```
#VampireSprite class, init method
    y = 50 + self.lane * 100
    self.rect = self.image.get_rect(center = (1100, y))
-   self.health = 100
+   self.health = STARTING_HEALTH

    def update(self, game_window, counters):
    game_window.blit(BACKGROUND,
                        (self.rect.x, self.rect.y), self.rect)
    self.rect.x -= self.speed
    if self.health <= 0 or self.rect.x <= 100:
        self.kill()
        if self.rect.x <= 100:
            counters.bad_reviews += 1
    else:
+       if 30 < self.health * 100 // STARTING_HEALTH < 60:
            self.image = MED_HEALTH.copy()
        elif self.health * 100 // STARTING_HEALTH <= 30:
! #To Do: Change the image to LOW_HEALTH
        game_window.blit(self.image, (self.rect.x, self.rect.y))
```

The new part of the **if** statement tells the program
that if the health is above **0** to execute another test.
If health is greater than **60**, it tells the program
to set the regular **VAMPIRE_PIZZA** image.
The nested **elif** statement sets the
vampire pizza image to **MED_HEALTH**
if the health points are greater than **30**.

Now use **else** to change the pizza
vampire image to **LOW_HEALTH**
when it drops below **30**.

Ordering Conditionals

Take a look at the if statement that we just set up to see why the order of the tests matter.

```python
if self.health * 100 // STARTING_HEALTH > 60:
    self.image = VAMPIRE_PIZZA.copy()
elif self.health * 100 // STARTING_HEALTH > 30:
    self.image = MED_HEALTH.copy()
else:
    self.image = LOW_HEALTH.copy()
```

First, we test if health is greater than **60** points (**61–100**). If it is, the test stops there.

If the health is lower than **60**, the test continues and asks if health greater than **30** points. If it is greater than **30** (so any number between **31** and **60**), the test stops there.

If the health is lower than **30**, the **else** condition is applied.

You can think of this as a flowchart:

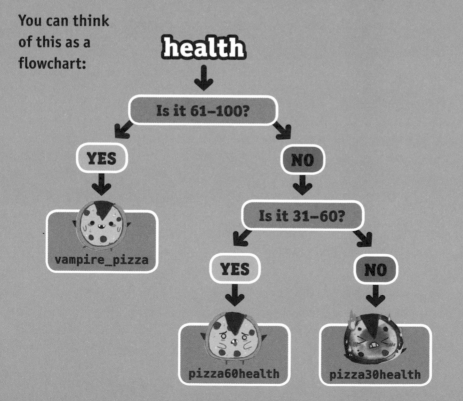

After you have made the modifications, don't forget to test and debug your modded game.

Add New Enemy Types

Right now there is only one type of enemy in our game: the vampire pizzas. Let's add three more enemies that have different behaviors. Adding new enemy types will create additional challenges for the player and increase the **re-playability** of the game. A game is re-playable when it is interesting to play multiple times. Adding variety helps keep a game interesting because players must adjust their strategy to different situations. In this case, they must learn to defeat new enemy types.

First we'll add a **werepizza**. This type of enemy moves faster than a vampire pizza.

1. Set up the image of the **werepizza** enemy type:

```
#Set up the enemy image
pizza_img = image.load('vampire.png')
pizza_surf = Surface.convert_alpha(pizza_img)
VAMPIRE_PIZZA = transform.scale(pizza_surf, (WIDTH, HEIGHT))
were_img = image.load('were_pizza.png')
were_surf = Surface.convert_alpha(were_img)
WERE_PIZZA = transform.scale(were_surf, (WIDTH, HEIGHT))

#Set up the tile trap images
```

2. Create a new **FAST_SPEED** variable:

```
#Define speeds
REG_SPEED = 2
SLOW_SPEED = 1
FAST_SPEED = 3

#-------------------------------------------------
#Load Assets
```

3. Create a subclass of **VampireSprite** called **WerePizza**.
Set the new starting speed and image in the **init** function:

```
#VampireSprite class, attack method
        if tile.trap == DAMAGE:
            self.health -= 1

class WerePizza(VampireSprite):
    def __init__(self):
        super(WerePizza, self).__init__()
        self.speed = FAST_SPEED
        self.image = WERE_PIZZA.copy()

class Counters(object):
```

4. Add an **attack** method in the **WerePizza** subclass that defines
how the enemy will react to the **slow** and **damage** traps:

```
#WerePizza class, init method
        self.speed = FAST_SPEED
        self.image = WERE_PIZZA.copy()

def attack(self, tile):
        if tile.trap == SLOW:
            self.speed = REG_SPEED
        if tile.trap == DAMAGE:
            self.health -= 1

class Counters(object):
```

5. In the section of your program where you created class
instances, add an empty list called **enemy_types**.
Then append **VampirePizza** instances and **WerePizza**
instances to the list:

```
#Create a sprite group for all the VampireSprite instances
all_vampires = sprite.Group()

enemy_types = []
enemy_types.append(VampireSprite)
enemy_types.append(WerePizza)


counters = Counters(STARTING_BUCKS, BUCK_RATE,
                    STARTING_BUCK_BOOSTER, WIN_TIME)
```

6. At the top of your program, import **choice** from **random**:

```
import pygame
from pygame import *
from random import randint
from random import randint, choice


pygame.init()


clock = time.Clock()
```

7. Replace the **VampireSprite()** instance with a command
that randomly chooses a type from the list **enemy_types**
and creates an instance.

```
                trap_applicator.select_tile(
                        tile_grid[y // 100][x // 100], counters)

#-----------------------------------------------
#Create VampireSprite instances
    if randint(1, SPAWN_RATE) == 1:
        VampireSprite()
        choice(enemy_types)()

#-----------------------------------------------
#Set up collision detection
    for tile_row in tile_grid:
        for tile in tile_row:
```

Stop and test your modified game. Debug until the **WerePizza** enemy type works as you intend.

Next, you can add a **zombie pizza**. This type of enemy comes back to life after it is destroyed once.

1. Set up the image of the **zombie pizza** enemy type:

```
were_surf = Surface.convert(were_img)
WERE_PIZZA = transform.scale(were_surf, (WIDTH, HEIGHT))

zombie_img = image.load('zombie_pizza.png')
zombie_surf = Surface.convert_alpha(zombie_img)
ZOMBIE_PIZZA = transform.scale(zombie_surf, (WIDTH, HEIGHT))

#Set up the tile trap images
```

2. If you haven't already, add **STARTING_HEALTH** to your game.

```
#Set up counters
STARTING_BUCKS = 15
BUCK_RATE = 120
STARTING_BUCK_BOOSTER = 1
STARTING_HEALTH = 100
```

3. Create a subclass of **VampireSprite** called **ZombiePizza**. Set the new starting health and image in the **init** function:

```
#WerePizza class, attack method
        self.speed = FAST_SPEED
        self.image = WERE_PIZZA.copy()

class ZombiePizza(VampireSprite):
    def __init__(self):
        super(ZombiePizza, self).__init__()
        self.health = STARTING_HEALTH * 2
        self.image = ZOMBIE_PIZZA.copy()

class Counters(object):
```

4. Add an **update** function in the **ZombiePizza** subclass that defines how the enemy will change based on health points:

```python
class ZombiePizza(VampireSprite):
    def __init__(self):
        super(ZombiePizza, self).__init__()
        self.health = STARTING_HEALTH * 2
        self.image = ZOMBIE_PIZZA.copy()

    def update(self, GAME_WINDOW, counters):
        GAME_WINDOW.blit(BACKGROUND,
                         (self.rect.x, self.rect.y), self.rect)
        self.rect.x -= self.speed

        if self.health <= 0 or self.rect.x <= 100:
            if self.rect.x <= 100:
                counters.bad_reviews += 1
            self.kill()

        else:
            percent_health = self.health * 100 // STARTING_HEALTH * 2
            if percent_health > 80:
                self.image = ZOMBIE_PIZZA.copy()
            elif percent_health > 65:
                self.image = MED_HEALTH.copy()
            elif percent_health > 50:
                self.image = LOW_HEALTH.copy()
            elif percent_health > 35:
                self.image = ZOMBIE_PIZZA.copy()
            elif percent_health > 20:
                self.image = MED_HEALTH.copy()
            else:
                self.image = LOW_HEALTH.copy()
            GAME_WINDOW.blit(self.image, (self.rect.x, self.rect.y))

class Counters(object):
```

Take a Closer Look

The zombie pizza comes back to life at full health after being destroyed once. We can imagine that the zombie pizza starts at **100** health, is destroyed when it reaches **0** health, and comes back with **100** health. We get this effect by doubling the health to **200**. It gets sicker and sicker until it reaches **100**. Then it returns to the "full health" image. Then it gets sicker and sicker again until it reaches **0** health.

RIP

| 100 health points | 100 health points |

5. Append **ZombiePizza** to the **enemy_types** list:

```
#Create an empty list for the enemy types and append
#instances of each type to the list
enemy_types = []
enemy_types.append(VampireSprite)
enemy_types.append(WerePizza)
enemy_types.append(ZombiePizza)

counters = Counters(STARTING_BUCKS, BUCK_RATE,
                    STARTING_BUCK_BOOSTER, WIN_TIME)
```

6. You should already have **choice** imported at the top of your program.

7. Now the **ZombiePizza** enemy type is part of the list **enemy_types** that is selected at random when enemies spawn. There is no need to make additional changes to the game loop.

> Stop and test your modified game. Debug until the **ZombiePizza** enemy type works as you intend.

Now use the **Cthulhu pizza** to create your own enemy type. A **Cthulhu** is an octopus-headed monster that causes insanity just by looking at it! Do you want to make your new enemy spawn at a faster rate? Make it resistant to one of the trap types? Set its starting health higher so it requires more damage to destroy? Do you have other ideas? Use your own creativity to decide how you want this new enemy type to behave. Then use what you've learned so far to code the new behavior.

Follow the five steps below:

1. Set up the new sprite image.

2. Add any new variables.

3. Create a subclass of **VampirePizza**. Define any changes in the **init** function.

4. If the new subclass behaves differently than the VampirePizza in the **update** or **attack** functions, then add those functions to the subclass with the changes. (If one of them does not have any changes, you do not need to add it.)

5. Append this enemy type to the list called **enemy_types**.

> Don't forget to test and debug your game until your new **Cthulhu Pizza** enemy type works exactly like you want it to.

Now you know how to change the image of a sprite and add new enemy types. Use these new skills to mod *Attack of the Vampire Pizzas!* to make it your own.

Chapter 16

Hack Your Game

You can add new mechanics and features to your game with just a few additional concepts. Build timers to control effects, use collision-detection methods, incorporate key-press events, create multiple levels, and adjust probability. In this section, I will give you examples of what you can do with these hacks, but there are many different ways that you can use them once you know how they work.

These examples include detailed code comments. Programmers often find examples of a feature that they would like in someone else's code. They find the part of the program that controls the feature that they want and adapt it to their own program. Use the code comments as well as what you know about Python to use these examples. You can also learn more by looking at the documentation on the Pygame website.

> **Power Up:** Most code editors will let you search for words or lines of code by typing
>
> *ctrl + f:* `Ctrl` + `F` or *cmd + f:* `Cmd` + `F`
>
> Use the **Find** shortcut to search for the line of code directly above or below the place where you would like to make a change in your program.

Control Effects with Timers and Collision

Because the game loop runs so quickly, you may want to delay some actions in the game. To do this, you would need to delay the **kill()** function.

Below, I have added new types of trap. One is a wooden pizza separator. This is a **mine trap** that brings the health of the vampire pizza that touches it to zero and causes the vampire pizza to disappear in an explosion. I need to delay removing the vampire pizza so that the player can see the explosion. I've added an attribute called **despawn** to control the timing. I'm also adding a **projectile trap** that does damage every time a projectile hits the pizza.

To add a new trap, I have to find and change every part of my program that a new trap would affect.

Load new images

```
#Set up the tile trap images
pepperoni_surf = Surface.convert_alpha(pepperoni_img)
PEPPERONI = transform.scale(pepperoni_surf, (WIDTH, HEIGHT))

#Loads the mine trap image
table_img = image.load('pizza-table.png')
table_surf = Surface.convert_alpha(table_img)
TABLE = transform.scale(table_surf, (WIDTH, HEIGHT))

#Loads the mine explosion image
explosion_img = image.load('explosion.png')
explosion_surf = Surface.convert_alpha(explosion_img)
EXPLOSION = transform.scale(explosion_surf, (WIDTH, HEIGHT))

#Loads the cannon trap image
cannon_img = image.load('anchovy-cannon.png')
cannon_surf = Surface.convert_alpha(cannon_img)
CANNON = transform.scale(cannon_surf, (WIDTH, HEIGHT))

#Loads the anchovy image
anchovy_img = image.load('anchovy.png')
anchovy_surf = Surface.convert_alpha(anchovy_img)
ANCHOVY = transform.scale(anchovy_surf, (50, 50))

#Set up classes
```

Add the new attribute to enemy class

```
#VampireSprite class, init method
    self.rect = self.image.get_rect(center=(1100, y))
    self.health = 100
    #Creates the despawn_wait attribute
    self.despawn_wait = None

#This function moves the enemies from right to left and
#destroys them after they've left the screen
```

Control the timing of the enemy effect

```
#VampireSprite class, update method

#This function moves the enemies from right to left and
#destroys them after they've left the screen
def update(self, game_window, counters):
    game_window.blit(BACKGROUND,
                     (self.rect.x, self.rect.y), self.rect)
    self.rect.x -= self.speed
    if self.health <= 0 or self.rect.x <= 100:
        self.kill()
        if self.rect.x <= 100:
            counters.bad_reviews += 1
#Subtract health when an anchovy hits a pizza
    collided = sprite.spritecollide(self, all_anchovies, True)
    if collided is not None:
        for anchovy in collided:
            self.health -= 10
#If the sprite reaches the pizza box, this sets despawn_wait to 0
    if self.rect.x <= 100:
        counters.bad_reviews += 1
        self.despawn_wait = 0
#If the sprite has not reached the pizza box and its health is 0,
#despawn_wait holds the explosion image for 20 game loops
    if self.despawn_wait is None:
        if self.health <= 0:
            self.image = EXPLOSION.copy()
            self.speed = 0
```

```
            self.despawn_wait = 20
        game_window.blit(self.image, (self.rect.x,
                                         self.rect.y))
#When despawn_wait reaches 0, sprite disappears from
#the screen
        elif self.despawn_wait <= 0:
            self.kill()
#If despawn_wait has a value above 0, counts down by 1 each
#game loop
        else:
            self.despawn_wait -= 1
        game_window.blit(self.image, (self.rect.x,
                                         self.rect.y))
```

Apply the effect to the enemy

```
VampireSprite class, attack method
        if tile.trap == DAMAGE:
            self.health -= 1
#If a vampire pizza touches a mine trap, sets health to 0
        if tile.trap == MINE:
            self.health = 0
```

Create a class instance for the new trap type

```
VampireSprite class, update method
SLOW = Trap('SLOW', 5, GARLIC)
DAMAGE = Trap('DAMAGE', 3, CUTTER)
EARN = Trap('EARN', 7, PEPPERONI)
#The 'MINE' trap costs 10 pizza bucks and uses the TABLE image
MINE = Trap('MINE', 10, TABLE)
#The 'PROJECTILE' trap costs 8 bucks and uses the CANNON image
PROJECTILE = Trap('PROJECTILE', 8, CANNON)
```

Add the new trap button to the background grid

```python
            if column <= 1:
                new_tile = InactiveTile(tile_rect)
            else:
                if row == 5:
#Check if the column contains a button tile
                    if 2 <= column <= 4:
                    if 2 <= column <= 6:
                        new_tile = ButtonTile(tile_rect)
#Assign a trap button to each column in the range
                        new_tile.trap = [SLOW, DAMAGE, EARN]
                                        [column - 2]
                        new_tile.trap = [SLOW, DAMAGE, EARN, MINE,
                                PROJECTILE][column - 2]

                    else:
                        new_tile = InactiveTile(tile_rect)
                else:
                    new_tile = PlayTile(tile_rect)
            row_of_tiles.append(new_tile)
#Test for tiles with trap buttons and adds the trap images
#to those tiles.
            if row == 5 and 2 <= column <= 4:
            if row == 5 and 2 <= column <= 6:
                BACKGROUND.blit(new_tile.trap.trap_img,
                            (new_tile.rect.x, new_tile.rect.y))
            if column != 0 and row != 5:
                if column != 1:
                    draw.rect(BACKGROUND, tile_color, (WIDTH * column,
                            HEIGHT * row, WIDTH, HEIGHT), 1)

GAME_WINDOW.blit(BACKGROUND, (0,0))
```

Add the location of each new trap to a list

```
REG_SPEED = 2
SLOW_SPEED = 1

#Empty list for storing location of all cannon traps
cannon_coordinates = []
#Determine the rate at which anchovies spawn
FIRE_RATE = 60

#------------------------------------------------------
#Load Assets
```

```
#PlayTile class, set_trap method
        if trap == EARN:
            counters.buck_booster += 1
#Adds location of each PROJECTILE type trap as it is set
        if trap == PROJECTILE:
            cannon_coordinates.append((self.rect.x,
                                       self.rect.y))
```

Create a projectile class and sprite group

```python
#InactiveTile class
    def draw_trap(self, game_window, trap_applicator):
        pass


#Creates a class for projectiles based on the Sprite class
class Anchovy(sprite.Sprite):
#The cannon_coordinates list will be passed with the
#coordinate argument
    def __init__(self, coordinates):
#Uses the rules for all sprites
        super().__init__()
#Sets the sprite image and speed
        self.image = ANCHOVY.copy()
        self.speed = REG_SPEED
#Adds all instances to the sprite group
        all_anchovies.add(self)
#Creates a rect for each instance
        self.rect = self.image.get_rect()
#Uses the coordinates of traps in the list cannon_coordinates
#to set the starting location of each anchovy
        self.rect.x = coordinates[0] + 40
        self.rect.y = coordinates[1] + 40
#Creates an update method for the Anchovy class
    def update(self, game_window):
#Erases old image as anchovy sprites move across the screen
        game_window.blit(BACKGROUND, (self.rect.x, self.rect.y),
                         self.rect)
#Moves anchovy sprites to the right
        self.rect.x += self.speed
#Removes anchovy sprites after they move off the screen
        if self.rect.x > 1200:
            self.kill()
#Displays the image of anchovy sprites in their updated
#location on the screen
        else:
            game_window.blit(self.image, (self.rect.x,
                             self.rect.y))

all_vampires = sprite.Group()
```

```
#------------------------------------
#Create class instances

#Create sprite groups
all_vampires = sprite.Group()
all_anchovies = sprite.Group()

counters = Counters(STARTING_BUCKS, BUCK_RATE,
                    STARTING_BUCK_BOOSTER, WIN_TIME)
counters = Counters(STARTING_BUCKS, BUCK_RATE,
                    STARTING_BUCK_BOOSTER, WIN_TIME, FIRE_RATE)
```

Spawn projectiles

```
#Counters class, init method
#Counters get FIRE_RATE passed to it when an instance is created
class Counters(object):
    def __init__(self, pizza_bucks, buck_rate, buck_booster,
                 timer):
    def __init__(self, pizza_bucks, buck_rate, buck_booster,
                 timer, fire_rate):
#Creates fire_rate attribute
        self.fire_rate = fire_rate
        self.loop_count = 0
        self.display_font = font.Font('pizza_font.ttf', 25)
        self.pizza_bucks = pizza_bucks
```

```
#Counters class
    def increment_bucks(self):
        if self.loop_count % self.buck_rate == 0:
            self.pizza_bucks += self.buck_booster

#Creates update_cannon method in Counters class
    def update_cannon(self):
#Loops through every cannon trap on the screen and spawns
#anchovies on each cannon trap at a set rate
        for location in cannon_coordinates:
            if self.loop_count % self.fire_rate == 0:
                Anchovy(location)

    def draw_bucks(self, game_window):
```

```
#Counters class, update method
#Calls the update_cannon method every time the Counters
#class update method runs
        self.draw_bucks(game_window)
        self.draw_bad_reviews(game_window)
        self.draw_time(game_window)
        self.update_cannon()

#Set up the different kinds of traps
```

Update projectiles in the game loop

```
#Game loop, update displays
        for tile in tile_row:
            tile.draw_trap(GAME_WINDOW, trap_applicator)

#Loops through all the anchovies and runs the update method
    for anchovy in all_anchovies:
        anchovy.update(GAME_WINDOW)

    counters.update(GAME_WINDOW)
    display.update()
```

Use Key-Press Events

A key-press event is a block of code that runs based on some
kind of input. For example, the **MOUSEBUTTONDOWN** event listens
(or polls) for the mouse button to be clicked, then runs the code
connected to that event. You can add other events to your program
such as **KEYDOWN**, which will listen for a key press. Some of the
things you can do with key-press events include allowing the player
to move sprites, select game objects, or reset a timer.

The example below uses key-press events to allow players to
select a trap. This improves the game because it allows for faster
gameplay. The player can select a trap with one hand on the
keyboard and place it using the mouse with the other hand.
You can find the complete list of the keyboard variable names
at **pygame.org** in the "keys" section.

Check for the new event

```
            #Set up the background tiles to respond to mouse clicks
elif event.type == MOUSEBUTTONDOWN:
            coordinates = mouse.get_pos()
            x = coordinates[0]
            y = coordinates[1]
            tile_y = y // 100
            tile_x = x // 100
            trap_applicator.select_tile(
                        tile_grid[tile_y][tile_x], counters)
#Listens for key presses
            elif event.type == KEYDOWN:
#Tests if the 1 key was pressed
                if event.key == K_1:
#Selects the trap button at row 5, column 2
                    trap_applicator.select_tile(tile_grid[5][2],
                                                counters)
#Tests for each key and selects the trap buttons
                if event.key == K_2:
                    trap_applicator.select_tile(tile_grid[5][3],
                                                counters)
                if event.key == K_3:
                    trap_applicator.select_tile(tile_grid[5][4],
                                                counters)
                if event.key == K_4:
                    trap_applicator.select_tile(tile_grid[5][5],
                                                counters)
```

Run the Game Loop as a Function

You may want to add levels to your game. To add a level without
creating separate program files for each level, you will need to
run your game loop slightly differently for each level. You can do
this by putting the loop into a function and passing it different
arguments for each level. In this example, Level 1 will only have one
enemy type: vampire pizzas. Level 2 will add two more enemy types:
zombie pizzas and werepizzas. Since it will be more difficult to
defeat multiple enemy types, the player will also start Level 2
with more pizza bucks.

Import module

```
import pygame
from pygame import *
#Imports the randint
from random import randint
from random import randint, choice
pygame.init()
clock = time.Clock()
```

Create variables to pass into the game loop function

```
SPAWN_RATE = 360
FRAME_RATE = 60
STARTING_BUCKS = 15
LVL1_STARTING_BUCKS = 15
LVL2_STARTING_BUCKS = 25
BUCK_RATE = 120
STARTING_BUCK_BOOSTER = 1
```

```
all_vampires = sprite.Group()

#Creates an empty list for the enemy types and appends
#instances of each type to the list
lvl1_enemy_types = []
lvl1_enemy_types.append(VampireSprite)
lvl2_enemy_types = []
lvl2_enemy_types.append(VampireSprite)
lvl2_enemy_types.append(WerePizza)
lvl2_enemy_types.append(ZombiePizza)

SLOW = Trap('SLOW', 5, GARLIC)
DAMAGE = Trap('DAMAGE', 3, CUTTER)
EARN = Trap('EARN', 7, PEPPERONI)
```

Power Up: *Highlight the entire game loop and press* **tab** *to increase the indent of every line in the loop by four spaces.*

Move the game loop into a function

```
GAME_WINDOW.blit(BACKGROUND, (0,0))

game_running = True
program_running = True

#Creates a function with arguments for anything that
#will change for different levels
def run_level(enemy_list, start_bucks):

#Indent the entire loop 4 additional spaces:
    while game_running:
        for event in pygame.event.get():
            if event.type == QUIT:
                game_running = False
                program_running = False
#Indent continues...
            counters.update(GAME_WINDOW)
        display.update()
        clock.tick(FRAME_RATE)
```

Spawn different enemy types

```
#run_level function
            tile_y = y // 100
            tile_x = x // 100
            trap_applicator.select_tile(
                    tile_grid[tile_y][tile_x], counters)

    if randint (1, SPAWN_RATE) == 1:
        VampireSprite()
        choice(enemy_list)()
    for tile_row in tile_grid:
        for tile in tile_row:
```

Scope

In programming, variables have a scope. The scope of a variable describes where a variable is assigned a value in a program and controls where that value can be used or reassigned in the program. Your program and the classes and functions in your program all have their own space where variables can be created, assigned, and reassigned.

Using a value

```
display_font.render(score)
end_points = score + 10
```

score = 0

VS.

Reassigning a value

```
score = 100
score += 2
```

Variables assigned outside of a class or function are called global. You can use these variables anywhere in your program, but you can only reassign their value outside of a class or function. Variables assigned inside of a class or function are called local. You can only use or reassign these variables inside of the function where they were created.

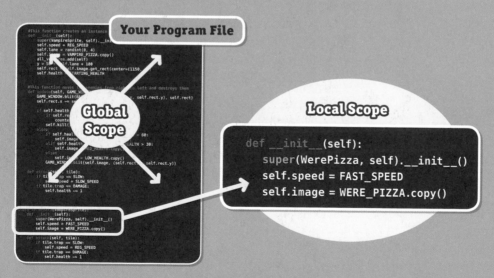

Your Program File

Global Scope

Local Scope

```
def __init__(self):
    super(WerePizza, self).__init__()
    self.speed = FAST_SPEED
    self.image = WERE_PIZZA.copy()
```

If you want to reassign a global variable inside of a function, you need to pass it in as an **argument**. If you want to use or reassign a local variable outside of a function, you need to **return** the value to pass it out of the function.

Imagine we own a pizza shop. We have a global variable that is the flour dough that we use for every pizza. We have functions that we use to run the recipe to make each pizza type. We have a cheese pizza function, a pepperoni pizza function, and a veggie pizza function. Each recipe function returns a type of pizza. If the pizzas aren't returned from the function, they can't go out to customers in the store. All the functions use the global dough to make their pizza. But some of our customers want whole wheat dough. We can't change the global dough variable to whole wheat or that would change everyone's pizzas to whole wheat and then we'd have angry customers! Instead, we can pass the type of dough into each recipe function as an argument. The function will make a pizza with the type of dough passed in and will return the pizza that the customer ordered. *Yum!*

Let's look at some pseudocode to see how this works in a program:

Global variable → `dough_choice = input ("regular or whole wheat?")`

Argument → `def pepperoni_pizza (pizza_dough):`
`    sauce = "tomato"`
`    cheese = "mozzarella"`

Assign the argument to a local variable → `pizza = pizza_dough + sauce + cheese`
`for range (20):`
`    pizza += pepperoni`
`pizza = 🍕`

Return the value of local variable → `return pizza`

Pass in global variable as an argument → `customer_order = pepperoni_pizza (dough_choice)`

`image.display(customer_order)`

Use returned value in global scope →

This will get you started with solving scoping problems in your programs. There are lots of other rules about scope in Python and other programming languages that you will learn as you continue to code.

Fix scope problems

```
all_vampires = sprite.Group()
counters = Counters(STARTING_BUCKS, BUCK_RATE,
                    STARTING_BUCK_BOOSTER, WIN_TIME)

SLOW = Trap('SLOW', 5, GARLIC)
DAMAGE = Trap('DAMAGE', 3, CUTTER)
```

```
        if column != 0 and row != 5:
            if column != 1:
                draw.rect(draw.rect(BACKGROUND, tile_color,
                    (WIDTH * column, HEIGHT * row, WIDTH, HEIGHT), 1)
```

```
GAME_WINDOW.blit(BACKGROUND, (0,0))
game_running = True
program_running = True
def run_level (enemy_list, start_bucks):
#Adds an argument called clear_tiles
def run_level (enemy_list, start_bucks, clear_tiles):
#Moves the background display into the run_level function
    GAME_WINDOW.blit(BACKGROUND, (0,0))
#Moves the counters instance into the run_level function
#and changes the first argument to take the variable
#passed into the second argument of run_level
    counters = Counters(start_bucks, BUCK_RATE,
                        STARTING_BUCK_BOOSTER, WIN_TIME)
#Clears all enemies from the display
    for vampire in all_vampires:
        vampire.kill()
#If the value of clear_tiles is True, clears all traps from
#the display
    if clear_tiles:
        for row in tile_grid:
            for column_index in range(len(row)):
                if isinstance(row[column_index], PlayTile):
                    row[column_index].trap = None
```

```
#Moves the running and waiting variables into the
#run_level function
    game_running = True
    program_running = True
    while game_running:
        for event in pygame.event.get():
            if event.type == QUIT:
                game_running = False
                program_running = False
```

```
        counters.update(GAME_WINDOW)
        display.update()

#Set the frame rate
        clock.tick(FRAME_RATE)
#Returns the value of variables to use outside of the function
    return game_running, program_running, counters
#End of game loop
```

Set up variables for level control loop

```
        display.update()
        clock.tick(FRAME_RATE)
    return game_running, program_running, counters

#End of game loop
#Creates a list of the arguments to pass in to the game
#loop function for each level
level_setup = [
    [lvl1_enemy_types, LVL1_STARTING_BUCKS],
    [lvl2_enemy_types, LVL2_STARTING_BUCKS]
]
#Sets the index for the current level to 0
current_level = 0
#Set up the end screen font
end_font = font.Font('pizza_font.ttf', 50)
#Sets program_running to True to start the while loop
program_running = True

if program_running:
    if counters.bad_reviews >= MAX_BAD_REVIEWS:
        end_surf = end_font.render('Game Over', True, WHITE)
```

Modify level control loop

```python
current_level = 0
end_font = font.Font('pizza_font.ttf', 50)
program_running = True
if program_running:
    if counters.bad_reviews >= MAX_BAD_REVIEWS:
        end_surf = end_font.render('Game Over', True, WHITE)
    else:
        end_surf = end_font.render('You Win!!', True, WHITE)
    GAME_WINDOW.blit(end_surf, (350, 200))
    display.update()

#Start of level control loop
#Clears traps from play tiles as long as it is not the
#start of the first level or end of the last level
while program_running and current_level < len(Level_setup):
    if current_level > 0:
        clear_tiles = True
    else:
        clear_tiles = False
#Stores the return values passed out of the level in
#global variables
    game_running, program_running, counters = run_level(
                level_setup[current_level][0],
                level_setup[current_level][1],
                clear_tiles)
#Tests if the lose condition was met and displays Game Over
    if program_running:
        if counters.bad_reviews >= MAX_BAD_REVIEWS:
            end_surf = end_font.render('Game Over', True, WHITE)
            game_running = False
            GAME_WINDOW.blit(end_surf, (350, 200))
            display.update()
#If it is not the final level, displays next level prompt
        elif current_level < len(level_setup):
            cont_surf = end_font.render(
                        'Press Enter for Level '
                        + str(current_level + 1), True, WHITE)
            GAME_WINDOW.blit(cont_surf, (150, 400))
            display.update()
```

```
#Creates a variable used to t   which end screen is displayed
        waiting_at_prompt = True
#Allows the player to exit the game from the end screen
        while waiting_at_prompt:
            for event in pygame.event.get():
                if event.type == QUIT:
                    waiting_at_prompt = False
                    program_running = False
#Creates a key-press event that triggers a loop that runs
#the next level of the game
                elif event.type == KEYDOWN:
                    if event.key == K_RETURN:
                        waiting_at_prompt = False
#If player did not lose the game and met the win conditions
#during the last level, displays 'You Won!!!' on the screen
        else:
            end_surf = end_font.render('You Won!!!')
            GAME_WINDOW.blit(end_surf, (350, 200))
            display.update()
#Changes the index of the current level by one after the
#key-press event
        current_level += 1
#Allows the player to close the game window from the
#win or lose screens
while program_running:
    for event in pygame.event.get():
        if event.type == QUIT:
            program_running = False
    clock.tick(FRAME_RATE)

#Clean up the game
pygame.quit()
```

Play with Probability

You can adjust a game by changing the chance that something in a range or list will be selected. You already adjusted probability when picking a random number from a range of numbers. For example, by increasing or decreasing the spawn rate, you can make it more or less likely that a vampire pizza will be spawned each time the game loop runs.

You can also adjust probability with the choice function by changing how often some items show up in the list that is being selected from. The example below makes it twice as likely that a vampire pizza will spawn than a werepizza in Level 1. In Level 2, a werepizza is more likely to spawn than a zombie pizza and a vampire pizza is more likely to spawn than a werepizza.

```
all_vampires = sprite.Group()

#Create an empty list for the enemy types and appends
#instances of each type to the list
lvl1_enemy_types = []
lvl1_enemy_types.append(VampireSprite)
lvl1_enemy_types.append(VampireSprite)
lvl1enemy_types.append(WerePizza)

lvl2_enemy_types = []
lvl2_enemy_types.append(VampireSprite)
lvl2_enemy_types.append(VampireSprite)
lvl2_enemy_types.append(VampireSprite)
lvl2_enemy_types.append(WerePizza)
lvl2_enemy_types.append(WerePizza)
lvl2_enemy_types.append(ZombiePizza)
SLOW = Trap('SLOW', 5, GARLIC)
DAMAGE = Trap('DAMAGE', 3, CUTTER)
EARN = Trap('EARN', 7, PEPPERONI)
```

Use Your Imagination and Coding Skills

The examples in this chapter are just one way to use each of these Python concepts. Think about other features or improvements that you'd like to add to your game. Use what you have learned about programming and the documentation on the **Python Software Foundation** and **Pygame** websites to make your own changes to the game.

Chapter 17

Explore New Games

You've programmed and customized *Attack of the Vampire Pizzas!* What comes next? That is up to you! This chapter is full of ideas to get you started.

If you want to make an entirely new game you can follow the same process that we used to create *Attack of the Vampire Pizzas!*

1. Plan out the game. Think about the elements of game design.

2. Break the game into parts.

3. Start by programming one part. Make changes and refactor as needed to make the parts work together.

4. Test and debug your game to make sure it works before you share it with others.

One-Button Side Scroller

What Is It?

A **one-button side scroller**, also known as an **infini-runner**, has one sprite that runs and jumps to avoid obstacles. Instead of the sprite moving forward, the background moves backward to give the impression that the sprite is running. The background objects spawn continuously, so the sprite never runs out of ground to cover.

How Does It Work?

In this example, a player controls a sprite with just one button as it flies along, avoiding cliffs and obstacles from above and below. If the sprite falls to the bottom of the screen or hits an obstacle, the player loses. If the sprite is able to avoid all obstacles for a given amount of time, the player wins.

Break It Apart!

Look at the screenshot of this one-button side scroller and think about all the different parts. You can't see all the game elements in a picture. Think about what is happening "behind the scenes."

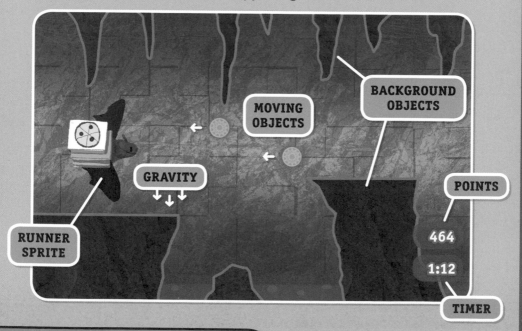

MOVING OBJECTS

BACKGROUND OBJECTS

GRAVITY

RUNNER SPRITE

POINTS

464

1:12

TIMER

Background Objects

Look of the objects: The look can be shapes or images that create a platform and obstacles for the runner.

> **_Suggestion:_** Use the **pygame.draw** module or the **pygame.image** module to create the background object surfaces.

Background object class: The objects need to be a class of sprites with rules for how all background objects behave. Each object needs a **rect**.

> **_Suggestion:_** Create a class based on **sprite.Sprite**.

Movement of the objects: The objects need to move across the screen from left to right.

> **_Suggestion:_** Change the x-coordinate of each object in an **update** function.

Spawning and despawning the objects: The objects need to spawn off-screen on the right and be removed from the game after leaving the screen on the left.

> **_Suggestion:_** Spawn objects in the game loop by creating an instance of the background objects class. Use the **kill()** method to remove sprites based on their location.

The Runner

Look of the runner sprite: The runner can be a shape or image.

> *Suggestion:* Use the **pygame.draw** module or the **pygame.image** module to create the runner surface.

Runner class: The runner needs a **sprite class** that defines how the runner behaves. The runner needs a **rect**.

> *Suggestion:* Create a class based on **sprite.Sprite**.

Runner movement: The runner needs to jump up when the player presses a specific key.

> *Suggestion:* Use the **KEYDOWN** event to cause the runner's y-coordinate to change (or look up a jump formula).

Gravity: When the key is not pressed, the runner needs to fall at a certain rate.

> *Suggestion:* Have the y-coordinate change a small amount each game loop (or look up a gravity formula).

Hitting an obstacle: The runner needs to be able to detect if it hits a background object.

> *Suggestion:* Use **sprite.spritecollide** to detect if the runner touches a wall.

Ending the Game

Timer: There needs to be a game timer that tracks time passing. The timer should be displayed on the screen.

> *Suggestion:* Look back at the **Counters** class and **draw_timer** method to see how we created and displayed a timer using the frame rate.

Earning Points: The player should earn points based on how long the runner stays alive. The points should be displayed on the screen.

> *Suggestion:* You can use the same tools that you used for the timer to add points based on time passing and to display them to the screen.

Win detection: If the player stays alive for a set amount of time, the game should stop.

> *Suggestion:* Test if the timer has reached a specific amount of time.

Lose detection: If the player falls off the bottom of the screen or hits an obstacle, the game should stop.

> *Suggestion:* Test the location of the runner. Use **collide** methods to detect if the runner touches an obstacle.

End screen: There should be some type of feedback that tells the player if they won or lost the game.

> *Suggestion:* Look back at the **end game loop** to see how to end the game loop and display a second loop that shows the end screen.

Two-Dimensional Shooter

What Is It?

The main game mechanic in a **two-dimensional shooter** is shooting at enemies to defend some type of base. The game space is flat, so the sprites can only move up, down, left, and right.

How Does It Work?

In this two-dimensional shooter, a spaceship will shoot laser blasts and aliens invading Earth. The aliens will try to destroy the ship by dropping bombs. If the ship is destroyed by the bombs or the aliens reach Earth, then the player loses the game. The player earns points by shooting aliens. The game usually continues forever, getting more and more difficult as time passes. Players compete for high scores. You can also choose to create a win condition based on reaching a specific number of points.

Break It Apart!

Look at the screenshot of this two-dimensional shooter and think about all the different parts. You can't see all the game elements in a picture, so also think about what is happening "behind the scenes."

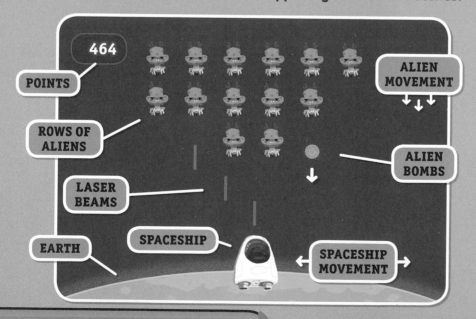

Spaceship

Spaceship sprite: Create a **class** for the spaceship sprite. The sprite should have a **surface**, a **rect**, and rules for how it behaves.

> **Suggestion:** Create a class based on **sprite.Sprite**. Use the **image.load** and **pygame.Surface.get_rect** to create the surface and the rect. Add functions to define the sprite's behavior.

Spaceship movement: The player should be able to move the spaceship right and left with key presses, using, for example, the arrow keys.

> **Suggestion:** Use **KEYDOWN** events to change the x-coordinate of the spaceship.

Laser beam sprites: The laser beams are **projectiles** that need their own **class** with a **surface**, a **rect**, and rules for how they behave.

> **Suggestion:** Create a class based on **sprite.Sprite**. Use the **image.load** and **image.get_rect** to create the surface and the rect. Add functions to define the sprite behaviors.

Firing laser beams: The player should be able to fire laser beams from the spaceship with a key press, using, for example, the space bar. The laser fire should be limited in some way, for example by limiting how many laser beams can be fired per second.

> **Suggestion:** Use a **KEYDOWN** event to spawn laser beams at the current location of the spaceship. Create a countdown timer that resets every time the laser is fired. Test if the timer is at zero before allowing more laser beams to spawn.

Laser beam behavior: Laser beams should move upward at a set rate. They should have rules for being removed from the game.

> *Suggestion:* Change the y-coordinate of laser beams every game loop. Use **spritecollide** or **collide_rect** to remove laser beams that hit an alien. Remove laser beams that move off the screen.

Spaceship hit points: The spaceship should have **hit points**. It should be able to detect when it has collided with an alien bomb. When a bomb hits it, some hit points should be taken away.

> *Suggestion:* Use **collide_rect** to detect when hit points should be taken away.

Aliens

Alien sprites: Create a **class** for the spaceship sprite. The sprite should have a **surface**, a **rect**, and rules for how it behaves.

> *Suggestion:* Create a class based on **sprite.Sprite**. Use the **image.load** and **image.get_rect** to create the surface and the rect. Add functions to define the sprite behavior.

Alien spawning and movement: Aliens should spawn in a set pattern from the top of the screen. Aliens should move across the screen in the pattern left, down, right, down, etc.

> *Suggestion:* Use a **nested loop** to spawn the aliens and control their movement (similar to the loop used to create the background grid in *Attack of the Vampire Pizzas!*).

Bomb sprites: The alien bombs are **projectiles** that need their own **class** with a **surface**, a **rect**, and rules for how they behave.

> **Suggestion:** Create a class based on **sprite.Sprite**. Use the **image.load** and **image.get_rect** to create the surface and the rect. Add functions to define the sprite behavior.

Bomb behavior: Bombs should spawn at random from alien sprites. Bombs should move down at a set rate and have rules for being removed from the game.

> **Suggestion:** Use **randint** to spawn bombs at the current location of each alien. Change the y-coordinate of alien bombs every game loop. Use **spritecollide** or **collide_rect** to remove bombs that hit the spaceship. Remove bombs that move off the screen.

Removing aliens: Aliens should be able to detect when they collide with a laser beam or with the ground. Aliens should be removed from the game when they collide with a laser beam.

> **Suggestion:** Use **spritecollide** or **collide_rect** to detect if aliens are hit by laser beams or touch the ground. Remove aliens that are hit by laser beams.

Ending the Game

Player points: The player should earn points for killing aliens. Points should be displayed on the screen.

> **Suggestion:** When a laser beam collides with an alien, add points to the player's total. Look back at any of the draw methods in the **Counters** class to use as a guide for displaying points.

Lose Condition: If an alien touches the ground or the spaceship is destroyed, the game should stop.

> *Suggestion:* Test if the spaceship's hit points are less than zero or if an alien has a y-coordinate that is off of the bottom of the screen.

Win Condition (optional): The game can end when the player reaches a certain number of points.

> *Suggestion:* Test if the player's points are greater than or equal to the number of points required to win.

End screen: There should be some type of feedback that tells the player how many points they ended with.

> *Suggestion:* Look back at the **end game loop** to see how to end the game loop and display a second loop that shows the end screen.

Top-Down Action Game

What Is It?

In top-down action games, the player is looking down on the sprites from up above. The type of top-down game that you will be thinking about has a sprite that tries to move from the bottom of the screen to the top of the screen but has to dodge several rows of moving objects to get safely to the other side. For example, the sprite could be crossing a busy highway.

How Does It Work?

In this game there are safe zones across the top and bottom of the screen. There are five rows in between the safe zones. In each row, there are objects continuously moving either from the right side of the screen to the left side or from the left side of the screen to the right.

The player controls the sprite with the arrow keys and can move one step at a time: forward, back, left, and right. To win, the player must get from one side to the other without getting hit by any of the objects and before the timer runs out. If the player is hit by an object or the timer runs out, they lose the game.

Break It Apart!

▶ **Your Turn**

Read the description and look at the screenshot of this top-down action game. Think about all the different parts, including what is happening "behind the scenes."

It's your job to break each section into smaller parts and to think about how you might program each smaller part. You can build this game with just what you've learned from this book.

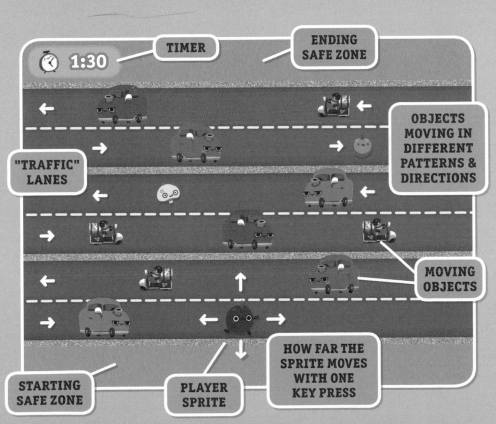

TIMER · 1:30

ENDING SAFE ZONE

OBJECTS MOVING IN DIFFERENT PATTERNS & DIRECTIONS

"TRAFFIC" LANES

MOVING OBJECTS

HOW FAR THE SPRITE MOVES WITH ONE KEY PRESS

STARTING SAFE ZONE

PLAYER SPRITE

Player Sprite

How will you set up the look and behavior of this sprite?

How will the player control the sprite?

How does the sprite move?

How does a sprite detect when an object hits it?

What happens to the sprite if it is hit by an object?
If it makes it to safety?

Suggestion: Use a **Pygame event type** to control the sprite.

Game Space

How will you create the safe spaces? How will you store information about where the safe spaces are? How will you detect if the player sprite reaches a safe space?

How will you create the traffic lanes? How will you store information about where the traffic lanes are?

How will you set a time limit on the game? How will you give feedback to the player about how much time they have to complete the game?

Suggestion: Use what you know about making a **background grid** to make background rows.

Moving Objects

How will you set up the look and behavior of these objects?

Where will the objects spawn?
Will they spawn in a pattern or at a set rate?

How will the objects move?

Do you ever need to remove objects from the game? If so, how?

How will the objects detect if they hit the player sprite? What happens if they hit the player sprite?

Suggestion: When you spawn objects, you can create a set spawning pattern or randomly spawn them at a certain rate. Have the objects in each row spawn differently. Think about how to make it most challenging (but still achievable) for the player to cross the lanes to the safe zone.

Ending the Game

How will you test if the player won the game? What will happen when the player wins?

How will you test if the player loses the game? What will happen if the player loses?

How will you give the player feedback about if they won or lost the game?

Suggestion: Use the **Pygame collision functions** to detect and get information about collisions.

Keep Calm and Code On

What ideas do you have? You know the major programming concepts and how to find the patterns in Python code. You can break games into programmable parts. You have lots of practice debugging. You can code your own game! What will you code next?

Appendix
Share Your Game

How to Share Your Game

Now that you've coded your own video game, it's time to find some players. You can choose to share your work with friends and family or with the whole world. There are a few ways that you can share it.

Easy Sharing

Your game is stored in files on your computer. The person you are sharing your game with needs to have Python and Pygame installed on their computer in order to run your game. The quickest way to share is to have the player use your computer or send the file to someone who has Python and Pygame installed on their computer. You can send your game by e-mail or put it on a thumb drive (*retro!*). Make sure to share the entire game directory, with all the asset files as well as your program file.

Advanced Sharing

If you want to share your game online, there will be more to learn! You can get permission from your parent or guardian to create an account on a development platform that allows sharing, like **GitHub.** It can take some time to learn how to use platforms like this, but once you do, you can post a link to your program anywhere. Other people who have Python and Pygame installed will be able to download and run your program.

Other Ways to Share

With permission from your parent or guardian, you can livestream or screen-capture yourself playing your game and post the video for others to see. You can post the code next to it or just write a description of the game.

Share Like a Pro

Give Attribution

When you share your program, make sure to give attribution. That means giving credit to other works on which your game is based. You can give attribution in code comments or text about your game. If you used any assets (images, video, music, sounds), you should say who created them or where you found them. If you find assets online, make sure that they are licensed for using and sharing. If you followed a tutorial or remixed large chunks of code from another program, then say who wrote the tutorial or program.

Protect Your Work

You can decide if and how other people can use your code. Many programmers make their code open-source. This means that other people can see it, use it, and remix it for free with attribution. If you want to, you can even find free licenses for open-source software online, such as the **Open Source Initiative.**

Security

Security is about protecting yourself and your computer from attacks, like viruses, malware, identity theft, or other harm.

Ideas to protect your security when sharing your game:

❊ Only download files from trusted websites. If you aren't sure if you can trust a source, ask a parent or guardian.

❊ Do not click on links or open messages from unknown people or if the subject line or link name doesn't look like something a friend would send you, like an advertisement.

❊ Create secure passwords and don't share them with anyone. Secure passwords don't include any personal information—not even your cat's name!

Privacy is about protecting your personal data. Personal data is information about you like your address, where you go to school, and your social security number. Personal data also includes information like what websites you visit, what video games you play, and your personal beliefs and opinions.

Ideas to protect your privacy when sharing your game:

❊ Educate yourself about how your data is collected, who collects it, and what that data is. To get started, check out:

   Electronic Frontier Foundation eff.org

   Me and My Shadow myshadow.org

❊ Choose what information needs to be kept private and what information you are comfortable sharing. Discuss your thoughts with a parent or guardian.

❊ Choose your audience. Choose how you will share your game based on which types of people you want to see your post and which types you don't.

Appendix
Keep Coding

If you enjoy programming, this book is just the beginning!

How to Learn More

The keys to learning to code:

❄ Try things when you are not sure if they will work.

❄ Be okay with making lots of mistakes.

❄ Keep trying again.

❄ Use code to make things that are fun and that you care about.

You can practice these skills in any programming language and any type of project.

Where to Learn More

Think about how you like to learn best. Do you prefer to learn by yourself or in a group? Do you like specific directions and instant feedback or do you prefer to work toward an interesting project and look up information as you need it?

Here are some ideas for learning more based on different learning preferences.

STRUCTURED

Structured and Independent

Learn on your own when you want, guided by a learning pathway.

- Interactive tutorials
- Online courses

INDEPENDENT

Self-Directed and Independent

Learn on your own and choose what you learn and when you learn it.

- Books and online tutorials
- Video tutorials • Just do it!

SELF-DIRECTED

> No matter what you choose, the most important thing that you can do to continue learning is to keep coding!

STRUCTURED

Structured and Collaborative

Learn in a group guided by an instructor.

- Coding Camps • After-school programs
- AP classes and school-based classes • Competitions

COLLABORATIVE

Self-Directed and Collaborative

Learn in a group and choose how and what you will learn.

- Hackathons and Makeathons
- Student clubs • Community meet-ups and events

SELF-DIRECTED

Appendix

Common Bugs

A **bug** is an error in your code. Bugs can cause the program to run in a way that the programmer didn't expect or intend or cause the program not to run and to throw an error message. **Debugging** is the process of finding and fixing errors. Debugging is a normal part of programming and game development. Here are some common bugs to look out for.

Off by One

Maybe the wrong list item is coming up or one of the columns in your grid isn't working. You might have an **off by one** error. This type of error occurs when you have one less than or one more than the number you needed.

Tips:

❋ Check to see if you started counting at 0.

❋ If you are using a range of numbers, does it include the first and last number in the range? Or does it exclude (not count) the first number, last number, or both?

❋ When you are testing if a total is greater than or less than a specific number, think about if you want to include that number by using greater than or equal to, or less than or equal to.

Example:

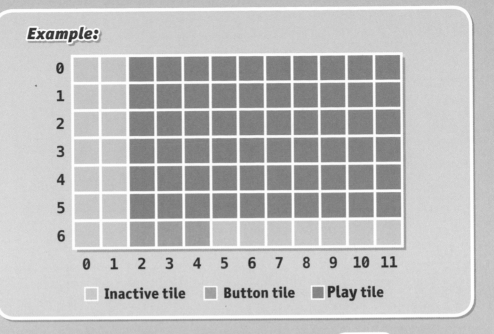

☐ Inactive tile   ☐ Button tile   ■ Play tile

BUG

```
for column in range(11):
    if column < 1:
        new_tile = InactiveTile(tile_rect)
    else:
        if row == 5:
            if 1 < column < 4:
                new_tile = ButtonTile(tile_rect)
```

DEBUGGED

```
    for column in range(11):
#This should be less than or equal to 1
#Now columns 0 and 1 will be marked inactive
        if column <= 1:
            new_tile = InactiveTile(tile_rect)
        else:
            if row == 5:
#This should be if greater than 1 or less than 5
#Now rows 2, 3, and 4 will be marked as buttons
                if 1 < column < 5:
                    new_tile = ButtonTile(tile_rect)
```

Forgot to Check for None

In Python, variables are labels that we put onto objects. Sometimes we can have a label with no object attached to it. When that happens, we use the word **None** to show that the variable has no value. We use None often in our game. For example, in our game, the PlayTiles have a trap value. If they don't have a trap, the value is None (no value). If they have a trap, the value is the trap type (earn, slow, or damage). When the trap returns a value, we can use the value to set that trap type on the background grid. We need to make sure that it won't cause an error if trap returns None (no value).

Tips:

✳ You can use **bool** to test if something has a value (True) or no value (False).

✳ Use **if statements** to run code only if a value is returned, making the test True. None will cause the test to be false and not run the code that would cause the error.

Example:

BUG

```python
#Tests for a collision and applies an effect
for vampire in all_vampires:
    vamp_left_side = vampire.rect.x // 100
    if -1 < vamp_left_side < 10:
        left_tile = tile_row[vamp_left_side]
    else:
        left_tile = None
vampire.attack(left_tile)
```

DEBUGGED

```python
#The attack function should only be called if
#left_tile has a value
#If we don't test if left_tile has a value, then running
#attack will cause an error every time left_tile is None *
    if bool(left_tile):
        vampire.attack(left_tile)
```

> ***Note:** We use **bool** in this tutorial to be clear about what is happening, but you can test for **True** or **False** with just `if variable_name:`.
>
> For example, `if bool(left_tile):` will give the same result as `if left_tile:`.

Spelling and Case

The program does exactly what you tell it. It doesn't have spell check or autocorrect. It looks for an exact match. It won't recognize words that are spelled wrong. It also won't recognize words that are capitalized when they shouldn't be or that are all lowercase when they should be capitalized.

Tips:

✳ If you get an error message that says a variable is not defined, go to the line number listed and check the spelling and capitalization of the variable. Does it match the created variable name exactly?

✳ Use File → Find to see if the name comes up in other places in your program. If it doesn't, then it is not an exact match.

✳ Check names character by character to see if they match.

Example:

BUG

```
class VampireSprite(sprite.Sprite):
    def __init__(self):
        super(vampiresprite, self).__init__()
        self.sped = REG_SPEED
```

DEBUGGED

```
#This code has two errors in it. It should read:
        super(VampireSprite, self).__init__()
        self.speed = REG_SPEED
```

Indentation Errors

The blank space in front of indented lines of code is called whitespace. Whitespace is made by either a space or a tab, but you can't see which by looking at it. Indentation errors happen when something is wrong with the whitespace. There might be too many spaces or not enough spaces.

Tips:

❋ Use the vertical lines in your code editor to do a visual check to see if anything is not lined up.

❋ It's easy to lose track of levels of indentation when you have several layers of nested loops or nested if statements. Check each nested layer. Comment out lines of code.

❋ If you see an error message that says "unexpected indent," find the line of code listed in the error message. Check the indentation on that line and on the lines above and below it.

❋ If the indentation looks correct, then you might have used spaces and tabs. If you indented one line with spaces and the next with tabs, you will get an error. Try using File → Replace to find all of the tabs and replace them with spaces.

Example:

BUG

```
if self.health <= 0 or self.rect.x <= 100:
    self.kill()
    if self.rect.x <= 100:
    counters.bad_reviews += 1
else:
    game_window.blit(self.image, (self.rect.x,
                        self.rect.y))
```

DEBUGGED

```
        if self.health <= 0 or self.rect.x <= 100:
            self.kill()
            if self.rect.x <= 100:
                counters.bad_reviews += 1
#This line should be indented four more spaces
        else:
            game_window.blit(self.image, (self.rect.x,
                                 self.rect.y))
#This line is indented five spaces instead of four
```

Other Syntax Errors

A syntax error happens when you don't match the exact pattern needed. It is very common to leave out important characters like a colon at the end of a line or have one of a pair of parentheses missing.

Tips:

✱ Find the line in your code from the error message. Check that line and the lines above and below it. Does each set of brackets or parentheses have matching pairs? Should the line end with a colon?

✱ Did you use one equals sign = to assign a value to a variable? Did you use two equals signs == to test if a value is True?

✱ If it's hard for you to focus on an individual line of code, try adjusting the settings of your code editor. Is it easier for you to read if the background is black instead of white? Would it help to make the font larger? What about holding up a piece of paper under the line of code that you are examining?

Example: BUG

```
if tile.trap = DAMAGE
        self.health -= 1
```

DEBUGGED

```
#The first line has two syntax errors. It should read:
if tile.trap == DAMAGE:
```

Name Not Defined

Your program is read and interpreted from top to bottom. If you try to use a variable before you define it, or if you try to call a function before you define it, the program will not recognize it.

Tips:

- If you get an error message that says something is not defined, check to see if you used that name above the place in the code where you defined it. Try commenting it out and moving it to another location.
- Organize your program. Keep your constant variables at the top of your program. Define all your classes and functions after the constant variables at the top of your program above the game loop.

Example:

```
SPAWN_RATE = 60
        if randint(1, SPAWN_RATE) == 1:
            choice(enemy_list)()
enemy_list = [VampireSprite, WerePizza, ZombiePizza]
#The program won't know where the enemy_list is because it
#reads the name enemy_list before the list is defined
```

Unable to Read the File

You might get an error related to an asset. If the program cannot load an asset, the problem might be with the file itself. It could be the wrong file type or the file might be corrupted in some way.

Tips:

* Check to see that the file name you typed in your code matches the name of the file exactly. Did you spell the file name right? Did you type in the right file type?

* Check the file itself. Is the file type supported by Pygame?

* Is the file in the same directory as your game file?

* Try running the program with a file that you know works. If it runs, you'll know there is something wrong with the file that you want to use. If it doesn't run, the error is likely related to your code.

Example:

```
#My file is called 'vampire.png.'
pizza_img = image.load( 'vampire.jpg' )
```

General Tips

* Did you save your changes in the code editor before running the file? You must save after every change.

* If you are getting an error message, read it.

* Take a break. Work on another part of your game or go do something else for a while and come back with fresh eyes.

* Try rubber duck debugging. Talk through the problem out loud. Explain it as if you are telling someone who might help you. If it helps, you can actually set an object like a rubber duck or an action figure next to your computer to talk to!

* Go back and use the strategies in the Grace's Corner boxes of this book.

* If you are working through this book with a friend or family member, try pair programming the section of code that you are struggling with. One of you will type and use the mouse (driver), the other one will direct what is typed (navigator). You can switch roles and talk it through together. Two sets of eyes are always better than one!

* You can ask the community for help on a forum. Get permission from a parent or guardian to post on forums. Asking for help is NOT asking other people to do your work for you. When you ask for help, post the segment of your code. Describe what is happening when you run the code. Describe what you have already tried and what you think the problem might be. Other people will want to help you if they can see that you have thought about the problem and are interested in learning.

Reading Error Messages

Error messages are not always easy to understand, but they provide information that can help you with debugging. Try these tips when reading error messages:

* Look for key words that you understand and connect them to what you know about programming.

For example, "unexpected indent" is probably related to indentation. A message with the words "not defined" is probably related to something that needs to be defined, like a variable or function name.

✱ Look for the line number in the error message. Find that line number in the code. First look at that line. Then look at any parts of the code related to that line of code.

✱ If you get a traceback error with many lines of code, start by looking for the error at the last line number given. It will be at the bottom of the error message.

✱ If you're using IDLE, you won't see any line numbers in your program file. To find a specific number, you can search for it by selecting **Edit → Go to Line**, or by using the shortcut **Alt + G**. You can also check the numbers on the bottom right corner of the file window.

Example:

The line number tells me where to look.

BUG

```
C:\ User/vampire_pizza_directory/VampirePizzaAttack.py
Traceback (most recent call first):
File "VampirePizzaAttack.py", line 30, in <module>
VAMPIRE_PIZZa = transform.scale (pizza_surf, (100, 100))
NameError: name 'pizza_surf' is not defined.
```

The problem is with this variable.

"Not defined" means we haven't assigned a value.

DEBUGGED

```
#The variable has no value because it is misspelled
VAMPIRE_PIZZA = transform.scale (pizza_surf, (100, 100))
#The error message gave us the clues to find and solve the bug
#without needing to understand every part of the message
```

Gallery of Downloadable Assets

Download these images and many more
at OddDot.com/codethisgame!

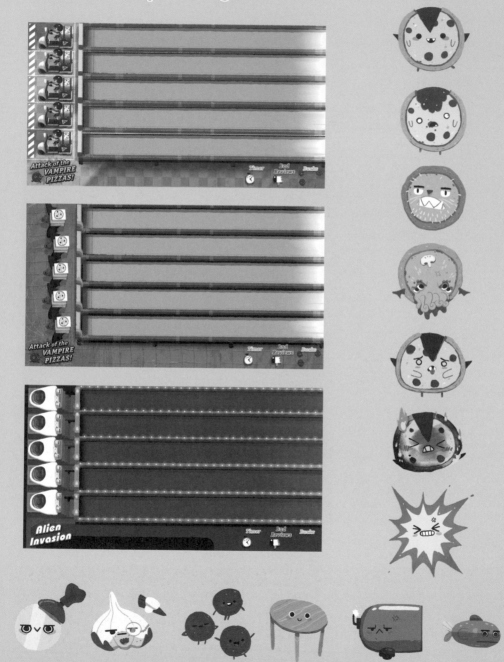

Index of Important Terms